The
Faith of a Writer

Also by Joyce Carol Oates

NOVELS

With Shuddering Fall (1964) · *A Garden of Earthly Delights (1967)* · *Expensive People (1968)* · *them (1969)* · *Wonderland (1971)* · *Do With Me What You Will (1973)* · *The Assassins (1975)* · *Childwold (1976)* · *Son of the Morning (1978)* · *Unholy Loves (1979)* · *Bellefleur (1980)* · *Angel of Light (1981)* · *A Bloodsmoor Romance (1982)* · *Mysteries of Winterthurn (1984)* · *Solstice (1985)* · *Marya: A Life (1986)* · *You Must Remember This (1987)* · *American Appetites (1989)* · *Because It Is Bitter, and Because It Is My Heart (1990)* · *Black Water (1992)* · *Foxfire: Confessions of a Girl Gang (1993)* · *What I Lived For (1994)* · *Zombie (1995)* · *We Were the Mulvaneys (1996)* · *Man Crazy (1997)* · *My Heart Laid Bare (1998)* · *Broke Heart Blues (1999)* · *Blonde (2000)* · *Middle Age: A Romance (2001)* · *I'll Take You There (2002)* · *The Tattooed Girl (2003)*

"ROSAMOND SMITH" NOVELS

Lives of the Twins (1987) · *Soul/Mate (1989)* · *Nemesis (1990)* · *Snake Eyes (1992)* · *You Can't Catch Me (1995)* · *Double Delight (1997)* · *Starr Bright Will Be With You Soon (1999)* · *The Barrens (2001)* · *Take Me, Take Me With You (2003)*

SHORT STORY COLLECTIONS

By the North Gate (1963) · *Upon the Sweeping Flood and Other Stories (1966)* · *The Wheel of Love (1970)* · *Marriages and Infidelities (1972)* · *The Goddess and Other Women (1974)* · *The Poisoned Kiss (1975)* · *Crossing the Border (1976)* · *Night-Side (1977)* · *A Sentimental Education (1980)* · *Last Days (1984)* · *Raven's Wing (1986)* · *The Assignation (1988)* · *Heat and Other Stories (1991)* · *Where Is Here? (1992)* · *Where Are You Going, Where Have You Been?: Selected Early Stories (1993)* · *Haunted: Tales of the Grotesque (1994)* · *Will You Always Love Me? (1996)* ·

The Collector of Hearts: New Tales of the Grotesque (1998) · *Faithless: Tales of Transgression (2001)*

NOVELLAS

The Triumph of the Spider Monkey (1976) · *I Lock My Door Upon Myself (1990)* · *The Rise of Life on Earth (1991)* · *First Love: A Gothic Tale (1996)* · *Beasts (2002)*

POETRY

Anonymous Sins (1969) · *Love and Its Derangements (1970)* · *Angel Fire (1973)* · *The Fabulous Beasts (1975)* · *Women Whose Lives Are Food, Men Whose Lives Are Money (1978)* · *Invisible Woman: New and Selected Poems, 1970–1982 (1982)* · *The Time Traveler (1989)* · *Tenderness (1996)*

PLAYS

Miracle Play (1974) · *Three Plays (1980)* · *Twelve Plays (1991)* · *I Stand Before You Naked (1991)* · *In Darkest America (Tone Clusters and the Eclipse) (1991)* · *The Perfectionist and Other Plays (1995)* · *New Plays (1998)*

ESSAYS

The Edge of Impossibility: Tragic Forms in Literature (1972) · *New Heaven, New Earth: The Visionary Experience in Literature (1974)* · *Contraries (1981)* · *The Profane Art: Essays and Reviews (1983)* · *On Boxing (1987)* · *(Woman) Writer: Occasions and Opportunities (1988)* · *George Bellows: American Artist (1995)* · *Where I've Been, and Where I'm Going: Essays, Reviews, and Prose (1999)*

FOR CHILDREN

Come Meet Muffin! (1998)

YOUNG ADULT

Big Mouth & Ugly Girl (2002)
Small Avalanches (2003)

An Imprint of HarperCollins*Publishers*

The Faith of a Writer

Life, Craft, Art

Joyce Carol Oates

 For information, address HarperCollins Publishers Inc., 10 East 53rd Street, New York, NY 10022.

HarperCollins books may be purchased for educational, business, or sales promotional use. For information, please write: Special Markets Department, HarperCollins Publishers Inc., 10 East 53rd Street, New York, NY 10022.

FIRST EDITION

Designed by Claire Vaccaro

Library of Congress Cataloging-in-Publication Data

Oates, Joyce Carol, 1938–
The faith of a writer : life, craft, art / Joyce Carol Oates.—1st ed.
p. cm.
ISBN 0-06-056553-5 (alk. paper)
1. Oates, Joyce Carol, 1938– 2. Oates, Joyce Carol, 1938—Authorship. 3. Authors, American—20th century—Biography. 4. Fiction—Authorship. 5. Authorship. I. Title.

PS3565.A8Z467 2003
813'.54—dc21
[B]

2003049235

03 04 05 06 07 BVG/RRD 10 9 8 7 6 5 4 3 2 1

to Daniel Halpern

CONTENTS

INTRODUCTION *xi*

MY FAITH AS A WRITER *1*

DISTRICT SCHOOL #7, NIAGARA COUNTY, NEW YORK *3*

FIRST LOVES: FROM "JABBERWOCKY" TO "AFTER APPLE PICKING" *13*

TO A YOUNG WRITER *23*

RUNNING AND WRITING *29*

"WHAT SIN TO ME UNKNOWN . . ." *37*

NOTES ON FAILURE *51*

INSPIRATION! *75*

CONTENTS

READING AS A WRITER: THE ARTIST AS CRAFTSMAN *93*

THE ENIGMATIC ART OF SELF-CRITICISM *127*

THE WRITER'S STUDIO *137*

BLONDE AMBITION:
AN INTERVIEW WITH JOYCE CAROL OATES
by Greg Johnson *143*

"JCO" AND I (*After Borges*) *153*

ACKNOWLEDGMENTS *157*

INTRODUCTION

Writing is the most solitary of arts. The very act of withdrawing from the world in order to create a counter-world that is "fictitious"—"metaphorical"—is so curious, it eludes comprehension. Why do we write? Why do we read? What can be the possible motive for metaphor? Why have some of us, writers and readers both, made of the "counter-world" a prevailing culture in which, sometimes to the exclusion of the actual world, we can live? These are questions I've considered for much of my life, and I've never arrived at any answers that seemed to me final, utterly persuasive. It must be enough to concede, with Sigmund Freud in his late, melancholy essay *Civilization and Its Discontents,* that "beauty has no obvious use; nor is there any clear cultural necessity for it. Yet civilization could not do without it."

Each of these essays, written over a period of years, represents a distinct facet of writing to me. Obviously, the so-called creative impulse begins in childhood, when we are all enthusiastic artists, and so I've included several essays about childhood experiences and predilections. Since writing is ideally a balance between the private vision and the public world, the one passionate and often inchoate, the other formally constructed, quick to categorize and assess, it's necessary to think of this art as a craft. Without craft, art remains private. Without art, craft is merely hackwork. The majority of the essays deal with this issue, most explicitly in "Reading as a Writer: The Artist as Craftsman" which focuses upon several works of fiction in analytic detail. Young or beginning writers must be urged to read widely, ceaselessly, both classics and contemporaries, for without an immersion in the history of the craft, one is doomed to remain an amateur: an individual for whom enthusiasm is ninety-nine percent of the creative effort.

Because writing is solitary, and yet an art, we can "learn" something about it; though fuelled by the unconscious, we can make ourselves "conscious" and even rather canny—to a degree. Certainly we can learn from others' mistakes, not only our own. We can be inspired by others' inspirations. In the essays "Notes on Failure," "Inspiration!" and "The Enigmatic Art of Self-Criticism" I've suggested a commonality of psychological/aesthetic issues perhaps unsuspected by the individual writers (Henry James, James Joyce, Virginia Woolf among others) who saw themselves, as most of us do, as solitary in their efforts. And there is the eerie dislocation of identity that all writers come to feel, especially with time: that we both are, and are not, our writing selves (" 'JCO' and I").

When did you know that you were going to be a writer? is a question writers are frequently asked. To me, the very question is a riddle, unanswerable. My instinct is to shrink from it: the assumption that I think of myself as a "writer" in any formally designated, pretentious sense. I hate the oracular voice, the inflated self-importance of the Seer. Bad as it is to encounter it in the world, it's worse to encounter it in oneself!

The spirit of *The Faith of a Writer* is meant to be undogmatic, provisional. More about the process of *writing* than the uneasy, uncertain position of being a *writer*. In my life as a citizen as in my life as a writer I have never wished to raise any practice of mine into a principle for others. Underlying all these essays is my prevailing sense of wonderment at how the solitary yields to the communal, if only, sometimes, posthumously. We begin as loners, and some of us are in fact con genitally lonely; if we persevere in our art, and are not discouraged in our craft, we may find solace in the mysterious counter-world of literature that transcends artificial borders of time, place, language, national identity. Out of the solitariness of the individual this culture somehow emerges, variegated, ever-alluring, ever-evolving.

March 2003

The Faith of a Writer

MY FAITH AS A WRITER

I believe that art is the highest expression of the human spirit.

I believe that we yearn to transcend the merely finite and ephemeral; to participate in something mysterious and communal called "culture"—and that this yearning is as strong in our species as the yearning to reproduce the species.

Through the local or regional, through our individual voices, we work to create art that will speak to others who know nothing of us. In our very obliqueness to one another, an unexpected intimacy is born.

The individual voice is the communal voice.

The regional voice is the universal voice.

DISTRICT SCHOOL #7, NIAGARA COUNTY, NEW YORK

As a child I took for granted what seems wonderful to me now: that, from first through fifth grades, during the years 1943–1948, I attended the same single-room schoolhouse in western New York that my mother, Carolina Bush, had attended twenty years before. Apart from the introduction of electricity in the early 1940s, and a few minor improvements, not including indoor plumbing, the school had scarcely changed in the intervening years. It was a roughhewn, weatherworn, uninsulated woodframe building on a crude stone foundation, built around the turn of the century near the crossroads community of Millersport, twenty-five miles north of Buffalo and seven miles south of Lockport. *I loved my first school!*—so I have often said, and possibly this is true.

In late August, in anticipation of school beginning immediately after Labor Day in September, I would walk the approximate mile from our house, carrying my new pencil box and lunch pail, to sit on the front, stone step of the school building. Just to sit there, dreamy in anticipation of school starting; possibly to enjoy the solitude and quiet, which would not prevail once school started.

(Perhaps no one recalls pencil boxes? They were of about the size of a lunch pail, with several drawers that, slid out, revealed freshly sharpened yellow "lead" pencils, Crayola crayons, erasers, compasses. Lunch pails, which perhaps no one recalls either, were of about the size of pencil boxes but, unlike pencil boxes, which smelled wonderfully of Crayolas, lunch pails quickly came to smell awfully of milk in Thermos bottles, overripe bananas, baloney sandwiches, and waxed paper.)

The school, more deeply imprinted in my memory than my own child-face, was set approximately thirty feet back from a pebble-strewn unpaved road, Tonawanda Creek Road; it had six tall, narrow windows in its side walls, and very small windows in its front wall; a steeply slanting shingleboard roof that often leaked in heavy rain; and a shadowy, smelly, shed-like structure at the front called the "entry"; nothing so romantic as a cupola with a bell to be rung, to summon pupils inside. (Our teacher Mrs. Dietz, standing Amazon-like in the entry doorway, rang a hand bell. This was a sign of her adult authority, the jarring noise of the bell, the thrusting, hacking gesture of her muscled right arm as she vigorously shook it.) Behind the school, down a slope of briars and jungle-like vegetation, was the "crick"—the wide, often muddy, fast-moving Tonawanda Creek, where pupils were forbidden to play or explore; on both sides of the school were vacant, overgrown fields; "out back" were crudely built wooden outhouses, the boys' to the left and the girls' to the right, with drainage, raw sewage, virulently fetid in warm weather, seeping out into the creek. (Elsewhere, off the creek bank, children, mostly older boys, swam. There was not much consciousness of "polluted" waters in those days and yet less fastidiousness on the part of energetic farm boys.)

At the front of the school, and to the sides, was an improvised playground of sorts, where we played such improvised games as "May I?"—which involved "baby-" and "giant-steps"—and "Pom-Pom-Pullaway" which was more raucous, and rougher, where one might be dragged across an expanse of cinders, even thrown down into the cinders. And there was "Tag" which was my favorite game, at which I excelled since I could run, even at a young age, out of necessity, fast.

Joyce runs like a deer! certain of the boys, chasing me, as they chased other younger children, to bully and terrorize us, and for fun, would say, admiring.

Inside, the school smelled smartly of varnish and wood smoke from the potbellied stove. On gloomy days, not unknown in upstate New York in this region south of Lake Ontario and east of Lake Erie, the windows emitted a vague, gauzy light, not much reinforced by ceiling lights. We squinted at the blackboard, that seemed far away since it was on a small platform, where Mrs. Dietz's desk was also positioned, at the front, left of the room. We sat in rows of seats, smallest at the front, largest at the rear, attached at their bases by metal runners, like a toboggan; the wood of these desks seemed beautiful to me, smooth and of the red-burnished hue of horse chestnuts. The floor was bare wooden planks. An American flag hung limply at the far left of the blackboard and above the blackboard, running across the front of the room, designed to draw our eyes to it avidly, worshipfully, were paper squares showing that beautifully shaped script known as Parker Penmanship.

Mrs. Dietz, of course, had mastered the art of penmanship. She wrote our vocabulary and spelling lists on the blackboard, and we learned to imitate her. We learned to "diagram" sentences with the solemn precision of scientists articulating chemical equations. We learned to read by reading aloud, and we learned to spell by spelling aloud. We memorized, and we recited. Our textbooks were rarely new, but belonged to the school district and were passed on, year after year until they wore out entirely. Our "library" was a shelf or two of books including a Webster's dictionary, which fascinated me: a book containing *words!* A treasure of secrets this seemed to me, available to anyone who cared to look into it.

My earliest reading experiences, in fact, were in this dictionary. We had no dictionary at home until, winner of a spelling bee sponsored by the *Buffalo Evening News,* when I was in fifth grade, I was given a dictionary like the one at school. This, like the prized *Alice* books, remained with me for decades.

My early "creative" experiences evolved not from printed books, but from coloring books, predating my ability to read. I did not learn to read until I was in first grade, and six years old, though by this time I had already produced numerous "books" of a kind by drawing, coloring, and scribbling in tablets, in what I believed to be a convincing imitation of adults. My earliest fictional characters were zestfully if crudely drawn, upright chickens and cats engaged in various dramatic confrontations; the title of my first full-length novel, on tablet paper, was *The Cat House.* (Somewhere, *The Cat House* still exists. Through my life, I seem to have been an unlikely combination of precocity and naiveté.)

After I learned to read, most of my reading was related to school, except for a few books we had at home, including the daunting *The Gold Bug and Other Stories* by Edgar Allan Poe, my father's book. What I could make of this, I can't imagine. Though Poe's classic tales would seem to move, in our memories, with the nightmare ease of horror films, yet the prose in which Poe cast these tales is highly formal, tortuous, turgid if not opaque. Yet, somehow, I persevered; I "read" Edgar Allan Poe as a young child, and who knows what effect that experience has had upon me? (No wonder my immediate kinship with Paul Bowles, whose first story collection, *The Delicate Prey,* is addressed to his mother, who had read him the tales of Poe as a young boy.)

My child's logic, which was not corrected by any adult because it would not have occurred to me to mention it to any adult, was that the mysterious world of books was divided into two types: those for children, and those for adults. Reading for children, in our grade-school textbooks, was simple-minded in its vocabulary, grammar, and content; it was usually about unreal, improbable, or unconditionally fantastic situations, like fairy tales, comic books, Disney films. It might be amusing, it might even be instructive, but it was not *real.* Reality was the province of adults, and though I was surrounded by adults, as an only child for five years, it was not a province I could enter, or even envision, from the outside. To enter that reality, to find a way *in,* I read books.

Avidly, ardently! As if my life depended upon it.

One of the earliest books I read, or tried to read, was an anthology from our school library, an aged *Treasury of American Literature* that had probably been published before World War II. Mixed with writers who are mostly forgotten today (James Whitcomb Riley, Eugene Field, Helen Hunt Jackson) were our New England classics—though I was too young to know that Hawthorne, Emerson, Poe, Melville, et al. were "classics" or even to know that they spoke out of an America that no longer existed, and would never have existed for families like my own. I believed that these writers, who were exclusively male, were in full possession of *reality*. That their *reality* was so very different from my own did not discredit it, or even disqualify it, but confirmed it: adult writing was a form of wisdom and power, difficult to comprehend, but unassailable. These were no children's easy-reading fantasies but the real thing, voices of adult authenticity. I forced myself to read for long minutes at a time, finely printed prose on yellowed, dog-eared pages, retaining very little but utterly captivated by the strangeness of another's voice sounding in my ear. I tackled such a book as I would tackle a tree (a pear tree, for instance) difficult to climb. I must have felt almost physically challenged by lengthy, near-impenetrable paragraphs so unlike the American-English language spoken in Millersport, New York, and unlike the primer sentences of our schoolbooks. The writers were mere names, words. And these words were exotic: "Washington Irving"—"Benjamin Franklin"—"Nathaniel Hawthorne"—"Herman Melville"—"Ralph Waldo Emerson"—"Henry David Thoreau"—"Edgar Allan Poe"—"Samuel Clemens." There was no Emily Dickinson in this anthology, I would not read Dickinson until high school. I did not think of these exalted individuals as actual men, human beings like my father and grandfather who might have lived and breathed; the writing attributed to them was them. If I could not always make sense of what I read, I knew at least that it was true.

It was the first-person voice, the (seemingly) unmediated voice, that struck me as *truth-telling*. For some reason, very few books for children are in the first-person voice; Lewis Carroll's Alice is always seen from a little distance, as "Alice." But many of the adult writers whom I struggled to read wrote in the first person, and very persuasively. I could not have distinguished between the (nonfiction) voices of Thoreau and Emerson and the (wholly fictional) voices of Irving and Poe; even today, I have to think to recall whether "The Imp of the Perverse" is a confessional essay, as it sets itself up to be, or one of the *Tales of the Grotesque*. I may have absorbed from Poe the predilection for moving fluidly through genres, and grounding the surreal in the seeming "reality" of an earnest, impassioned voice. Poe was a master of, among other things, the literary trompe l'oeil, in which speculative musings upon human psychology shift into fantastic narratives while retaining the same first-person voice.

I would one day wonder why the earliest, most "primitive" forms of art seem to have been fabulist, legendary, and surreal, populated not by ordinary, life-sized men and women but by gods, giants, and monsters? Why was reality so slow to evolve? It's as if, looking into a mirror, our ancestors shrank from seeing their own faces in the hope of seeing something other—exotic, terrifying, comforting, idealistic, or delusional—but distinctly *other*.

Of Mrs. Dietz, I think: how heroic she must have been!

Underpaid, undervalued, overworked. Not only was it the task of a one-room schoolteacher to lead eight disparate grades through their lessons, but to maintain discipline in the classroom, where most of the older boys attended school grudgingly, waiting for their sixteenth birthdays when they were legally released from attending school and could work with their fathers on family farms; these boys were taught by their fathers to hunt and kill animals, and they were without mercy in "teasing" (the term "harassing" hadn't yet been coined) younger children. (Some of this "teasing" could become very cruel. Certainly, out of Mrs. Dietz's earshot, it shaded into what would be called in a more civil environment "assault" and "sexual molestation"—but that's another story, at odds with the romance of childhood nostalgia.) Mrs. Dietz was also in charge of maintaining our woodburning stove, the school's only source of heat, in that pitiless upstate New York climate in which below-zero temperatures weren't uncommon on gusty winter mornings, and we had to wear mittens, hats, and coats through the day, stamping our booted feet against the drafty plank floor to keep our toes from going numb. . . . I can only imagine the physical as well as the emotional and psychological difficulties poor Mrs. Dietz endured, and feel now a belated kinship with her, who had seemed to me a very giantess of my childhood. No other teacher looms as archetypal in my memory, for no other teacher taught me the fundamental skills of reading, writing, and "doing" arithmetic, that seem to me as natural as breathing. I am grateful to Mrs. Dietz for not (visibly) breaking down, and for maintaining a certain degree of good cheer in the classroom. The schoolhouse for all its shortcomings and dangers became for me a kind of sanctuary: a precious counter-world to the chaotic and unbookish roughness that existed outside it.

For a long time vacant and boarded-up, District #7 school was finally razed about twenty years ago. And for a long time afterward, when I returned to Millersport to visit my parents, I would make a sentimental pilgrimage to the site, where a wrecked stone foundation and a mound of rubble were all that remained. Soon such one-room schoolhouses will be recalled, if at all, only in photographs: links with a mythopoetic "American frontier past" that, when it was lived, seemed to us, who lived it, simply life.

FIRST LOVES: FROM "JABBERWOCKY" TO "AFTER APPLE PICKING"

There are two primary influences in a writer's life: those influences that come so early in childhood, they seem to soak into the very marrow of our bones and to condition our interpretation of the universe thereafter; and those that come a little later, when we are old enough to exercise some control of our environment and our response to it, and have begun to be aware not only of the emotional power but the strategies of art.

In 1946, for my eighth birthday, my grandmother gave me a beautiful illustrated copy of Lewis Carroll's *Alice in Wonderland* and *Through the Looking-Glass.* Out of nowhere this marvel came to me, a farm child, in a work-oriented household in which there were very few books and very little time for reading. My grandmother's gift with its handsome cloth cover embossed with bizarre creatures, and the perpetually astonished-looking Alice in their midst, would be the great treasure of my childhood, and the most profound literary influence of my life. This was love at first sight! (Very likely, I fell in love with the phenomenon of Book, too. I came to wonder what, or who, "Lewis Carroll" was, on the book's spine and title page.)

Like Alice, with whom I identified unquestionably, I plummeted headfirst down the rabbit hole and/or climbed boldly through the mirror into the looking-glass world and, in a manner of speaking, never entirely returned to "real" life.

You will remember that when Alice climbs through the looking-glass in her family's drawing room (not that Alice's "family" ever appears in the books: Alice is always wonderfully alone), into a drawing room that appears identical to the one she has left, she thinks with childish glee, "Oh, what fun it'll be, when they see me through the glass in here, and can't get at me!" And then, looking about, Alice realizes that "what could be seen from the old room was quite common and uninteresting, but all the rest was as different as possible. For instance, the pictures on the wall next to the fire seemed to be all alive, and the very clock on the chimney piece (you know you can only see the back of it in the Looking-Glass) had got the face of a little old man, and grinned at her."

My heroine was this strangely assured, rather reckless girl of approximately my age who I could not have guessed was of another culture and distinctly of another economic class; I most admired her for her curiosity, which was even greater than my own, and for the equanimity with which she confronted dream and nightmare situations, as I could not have done. Within a few weeks I had memorized much of both Alice books, and could recite, for anyone willing to listen, nearly all the poems.

(I still can. Sometimes waking in the night I scroll through them in sequence thinking how strange! how wonderful! the words of "Lewis Carroll" deceased since 1898 preserved, as Auden said with such memorable bluntness, in the guts of the living.)

The first *Wonderland* poem, which is the first poem of my life, looks, to a contemporary adult eye, like experimental verse by (for instance) e. e. cummings or William Carlos Williams. This curiosity, which fascinated me as a child and inspired me to much imitation, in Crayolas, on sheets of construction paper, has no title, and begins with the startling word "Fury." The poem replicates a mouse's long tail, dwindling down the page until its final, mordant words are set in

"Fury said to
a mouse, That
he met
in the
house,
'Let us
both go
to law:
I will
prosecute
you.
Come, I'll
take no
denial:
We must
have a
trial;
For
really
this
morning
I've
nothing
to do.'
Said the
mouse to
the cur,
'Such a
trial,
dear sir,
With no
jury or
judge,
would be
wasting
our breath.'
'I'll be
fury.'
Said
cunning
old. Fury:
'I'll try
the whole
cause,
and
condemn
you
to
death.' "

miniature type, scarcely readable. A mysterious, cruel poem for a child to decode, and to memorize, it blows up the miniature to the size of an epic, and makes of the injustice of cat/mouse relations something jokey. In the Alice books there is a yearning for justice and yet there is mostly injustice, a subversive text indeed. A classic for children that is also preoccupied with dying, death, and being eaten; perhaps more terrifying, being physically transformed into freakish shapes. The "Fury" poem is meant to be playful, its sympathy is for the doomed mouse, and yet: Fury is the victor, and has the final word. His anonymous mouse/victim, though illustrated in the book in a posture of appeal, is denied even a name.

Children's literature, especially in the past, did not shrink from depictions of cruelty and sadism; Lewis Carroll, in whom the child-self abided through his celibate lifetime, understood instinctively the child's nervous propensity to laugh at the very things that arouse anxiety: injustice, abrupt death, disappearing, being devoured. Most of the *Alice* poems appear whimsical until you examine them closely. Many depict abrupt outbursts of temper ("Off with his head!"—"Be off, or I'll kick you downstairs!") or inanities of adult judgment so extreme as to be comic:

Speak roughly to your little boy
And beat him when he sneezes;

He only does it to annoy,
Because he knows it teases.

The more blatant the rime, the more it appeals to a child's ear; as adults, we hear such rimes as mock-poetry, and one of the things they mock is adult subtlety and nuance.

But it was the sharply rimed and accented "Jabberwocky" that made the most profound impression on me. For young children, whose brains are struggling to comprehend language, words are magical in any case; the magic of adults, utterly mysterious; no child can distinguish between "real" words and nonsensical or "unreal" words, and verse like Lewis Carroll's brilliant "Jabberwocky" has the effect of both arousing childish anxiety (what do these terrifying words *mean*?) and placating it (don't worry: you can decode the meaning by the context). In *The Annotated Alice*, edited by Martin Gardner, footnotes for "Jabberwocky" cover several pages in small type; it's considered the greatest nonsense poem in English. I was fascinated by the bizarre, secret language and by the poem's dreamlike violent action, depicted in the most hideous of John Tenniel's drawings, of a grotesque winged monster with a tail like a python and gigantic claws, confronted by a very small boy with a sword. I must have liked it, thoughtful child that I was, to be told that, "vorpal sword in hand," the young hero rested "by the Tum-

tum tree, / And stood awhile in thought." The entire poem is irremediably imprinted in my memory, who knows why? It's a fantasy of a child's successful defense against the (adult) unknown, perhaps. It's a parody of heroic adventure tales. But I think, for me, it was the language that most fascinated: "One, two! One, two! / And through and through / The vorpal blade went snicker-snack! / He left it dead, and with its head / He went galumphing back."

How has Lewis Carroll's verse influenced my poetry? Has there been any direct influence at all? It may be that the *Alice* books have more influenced my philosophical/metaphysical perspective on life than my poetry. At the periphery of many of my poems and works of fiction, as in the corner of an eye, there is often an element of the grotesque or surreal. As a child as young as eight I may have been imbued with an indelible sense of playfulness and morbidity, in about equal measure. But isn't this, Lewis Caroll would inquire pleasantly, simply the way the world *is*?

Those poets I read, and reread, in high school, college, and in my early twenties have had a more obvious influence on my writing, of course. Of these, unquestionably, perhaps inevitably, Robert Frost was my first poet. Frost's influence is so pervasive in American poetry, like Whitman's, as to be beyond assessment. Like the verse of Lewis Carroll, the poetry of Frost has entered my soul. Frost's deceptively plain language, the subtle rhythm of his poetry, his beauty of phrasing, his irony and stoic resolve, are never in stronger evidence than in my favorite Frost poem, "After Apple Picking," which I read first in high school at about the age of fifteen. This poem of surpassing beauty and melancholy had a particular significance for me since I did pick apples, pears, and cherries in my family's fruit orchard, standing on a ladder, though I was never allowed to climb as high as my father on his "long two-pointed ladder." I understood from experience how the poet's "instep arch not only keeps the ache, / It keeps the pressure of a ladder-round." Frost allowed young writers like me to see that the experiences of our domestic, seemingly ordinary lives could be transmuted into worthy art; not Shakespeare's exalted kings and queens and nobility, in poetry so refined and intricate it seemed, to young readers, another language entirely, were his subjects, but men, women, and children like ourselves. This is a distinctly American poetry, accessible to anyone. It isn't the subjects we write about but the seriousness and subtlety of our expression that determines the worth of our effort.

"After Apple Picking" is a hypnotic, haunting poem. I was a teenager when I first read it, yet I could sympathize with its somber reflective lines, which are those of an older individual (a poet?) looking back upon his life with mingled pride and regret. The poem's powerful subtext is the inevitability of loss. I think I came closest to understanding Frost in the lines:

For I have had too much
Of apple picking: I am overtired
Of the great harvest I myself desired.

In its understated way the poem is a tragic work of art. Yet there remains a defiant human resilience beneath, as in us all.

TO
A YOUNG WRITER

W*rite your heart out.*

Never be ashamed of your subject, and of your passion for your subject.

Your "forbidden" passions are likely to be the fuel for your writing. Like our great American dramatist Eugene O'Neill raging through his life against a long-deceased father; like our great American prose stylist Ernest Hemingway raging through his life against his mother; like Sylvia Plath and Anne Sexton struggling through their lives with the seductive Angel of Death, tempting them to the ecstasy of self-murder. The instinct for violent self-laceration in Dostoyevsky, and for the sadistic punishment of "disbelievers" in Flannery O'Connor. The fear of going mad in Edgar Allan Poe and committing an irrevocable, unspeakable act—murdering an elder or a wife, hanging and putting out the eyes of one's "beloved" pet cat. Your struggle with your buried self, or selves, yields your art; these emotions are the fuel that drives your writing and makes possible hours, days, weeks, months and years of what will appear to others, at a distance, as "work." Without these ill-understood drives you might be a superficially happier person, and a more involved citizen of your community, but it isn't likely that you will create anything of substance.

What advice can an older writer presume to offer to a younger? Only what he or she might wish to have been told years ago. Don't be discouraged! Don't cast sidelong glances, and compare yourself to others among your peers! (Writing is not a race. No one really "wins." The satisfaction is in the effort, and rarely in the consequent rewards, if there are any.) And again, *write your heart out.*

Read widely, and without apology. Read what you want to read, not what someone tells you you should read. (As Hamlet remarks, "I know not 'should.' ") Immerse yourself in a writer you love, and read everything he or she has written, including the very earliest work. Especially the very earliest work. Before the great writer became great, or even good, he/she was groping for a way, fumbling to acquire a voice, perhaps just like you.

Write for your own time, if not for your own generation

exclusively. You can't write for "posterity"—it doesn't exist. You can't write for a departed world. You may be addressing, unconsciously, an audience that doesn't exist; you may be trying to please someone who won't be pleased, and who isn't worth pleasing.

(But if you feel unable to "write your heart out"—inhibited, embarrassed, fearful of hurting or offending the feelings of others—you may want to try a practical solution and write under a pseudonym. There's something wonderfully liberating, even childlike, about a "pen-name": a fictitious name given to the instrument with which you write, and not attached to *you*. If your circumstances change, you could always claim your writing self. You could always abandon your writing self, and cultivate another. Early publication can be a dubious blessing: we all know writers who would give anything to have not published their first book, and go about trying to buy up all existing copies. Too late!)

(Of course, if you want a professional life that involves teaching, lectures, readings—you will have to acknowledge a public writing name. But only *one*.)

Don't expect to be treated justly by the world. Don't even expect to be treated mercifully.

Life is lived head-on, like a roller coaster ride: "art" is coolly selective, and can be created only in retrospect. But don't live life in order to write about it since the "life" so lived will be artificial and pointless. Better to invent wholly an alternate life. Far better!

Most of us fall in love with works of art, many times during the course of our lifetimes. Give yourself up in admiration, even in adoration, of another's art. (How Degas worshipped Manet! How Melville loved Hawthorne! And how many young, yearning, brimming-with-emotion poets has Walt Whitman sired!) If you find an exciting, arresting, disturbing voice or vision, immerse yourself in it. You will learn from it. In my life I've fallen in love with (and never wholly fallen out of love from) writers as diverse as Lewis Carroll, Emily Brontë, Kafka, Poe, Melville, Emily Dickinson, William Faulkner, Charlotte Brontë, Dostoyevsky . . . In reading the new edition of Mark Twain's *Huckleberry Finn* not long ago, I discovered I'd memorized entire passages of this novel. In rereading the now virtually unread Studs Lonigan trilogy, by James T. Farrell, I discovered I'd memorized entire passages. There are poems of Emily Dickinson I probably know more intimately than Emily Dickinson herself knew them; they are imprinted in my memory in a way they would not have been imprinted in hers. There are poems of William Butler Yeats, Walt Whitman, Robert Frost, D. H. Lawrence that leave me chilled with excitement decades after I'd first discovered them.

Don't be ashamed of being an idealist, of being romantic

and "yearning." If you yearn for people who won't reciprocate your interest in them, you should know that your yearning for them is probably the most valuable thing about them. So long as it's unrequited.

Don't too quickly prejudge classics. Or contemporaries. Choose a book to read, now and then, against the grain of your taste, or what you believe is your taste. It *is* a man's world; a woman whose sensibility has been stoked by feminism will find much to annoy and offend, but perhaps there's much to learn, and to be inspired by, if only in knowing what it is to be an outsider gazing in. Such great works as Homer's *Odyssey* and Ovid's *Metamorphoses,* read from the perspective of the twenty-first century, the one primitive in its genius, the other unnervingly "modern," strike male and female readers in very different ways. A woman should acknowledge her hurt, her anger and her hope of "justice"; even a hope for revenge might be a good thing, in her work if not in her life.

Language is an icy-cool medium, on the page. Unlike performers and athletes, we get to re-imagine, revise and rewrite completely if we wish. Before our work is set *in print,* as *in stone,* we maintain our power over it. The first draft may be stumbling and exhausting, but the next draft or drafts will be soaring and exhilarating. Only have faith: the first sentence can't be written until the last sentence has been written. Only then do you know where you've been going, and where you've been.

The novel is the affliction for which only the novel is the cure.

And one final time: *Write your heart out.*

RUNNING AND WRITING

Running! If there's any activity happier, more exhilarating, more nourishing to the imagination, I can't think what it might be. In running, the mind flies with the body; the mysterious efflorescence of language seems to pulse in the brain, in rhythm with our feet and the swinging of our arms. Ideally, the runner-who's-a-writer is running through the land- and cityscapes of her fiction, like a ghost in a real setting.

There must be some analogue between running and dreaming. The dreaming mind is usually bodiless, has peculiar powers of locomotion and, in my experience at least, often runs or glides or "flies" along the ground, or in the air. (Leaving aside the blunt, deflating theory that dreams are merely compensatory: you fly in sleep because in life you crawl, barely; you're soaring above others in sleep because in life others soar above you.) Possibly these fairy-tale feats of locomotion are atavistic remnants, the hallucinatory memory of a distant ancestor for whom the physical being, charged with adrenaline in emergency situations, was indistinguishable from the spiritual or intellectual. In running, "spirit" seems to pervade the body; as musicians experience the uncanny phenomenon of tissue memory in their fingertips, so the runner seems to experience in feet, lungs, quickened heartbeat, an extension of the imagining self. The structural problems I set for myself in writing, in a long, snarled, frustrating and sometimes despairing morning of work, for instance, I can usually unsnarl by running in the afternoon. On days when I can't run, I don't feel "myself" and whoever the "self" is I do feel, I don't like nearly so much as the other. And the writing remains snarled in endless revisions.

Writers and poets are famous for loving to be in motion. If not running, hiking; if not hiking, walking. (Walking, even fast, is a poor second to running, as all runners know, that we'll resort to when our knees go, but at least it's an option.) The great English Romantic poets were clearly inspired by their long walks, in all weather: Wordsworth and Coleridge in the idyllic Lake District, for instance; Shelley ("I always go until I am stopped and I never am stopped") in his four intense years in Italy. The New England Transcendentalists, most famously Henry David Thoreau, were ceaseless walkers; Thoreau boasted of having "traveled much in Concord," and in his eloquent essay "Walking" acknowledged that he had to spend more than four hours out-of-doors daily, in motion; otherwise he felt "as if I had some sin to be atoned for." My favorite prose on the subject is Charles Dickens's "Night Walks," which Dickens wrote some years after having suffered extreme insomnia that propelled him out into the London streets at night. Written with Dickens's usual brilliance, this haunting essay seems to hint at more than its words reveal; Dickens associates his terrible night-restlessness with being unhoused, thus out of character; his new, impersonal identity he calls "Houselessness"—under a compulsion to walk, and walk, and walk in the darkness and pattering rain. (No one has captured the romance of desolation, the ecstasy of near-madness, more forcibly than Dickens, so wrongly interpreted as a dispenser of popular, soft-hearted tales.) It isn't surprising that Walt Whitman should have tramped impressive distances, for you can feel the pulse-beat of the walker in his slightly breathless, incantatory poems, but it may be surprising to learn that Henry James, who for all his prose style more resembles the fussy intricacies of crotcheting than the fluidity of movement, also loved to walk for miles in London.

I, too, walked (and ran) for miles in London, years ago. Much of it in Hyde Park. Regardless of weather! Living for a sabbatical year with my English professor husband in a corner of Mayfair overlooking Speakers' Corner, I was so afflicted with homesickness for America, and for Detroit, I ran compulsively; not as a respite for the intensity of writing, but as a function of writing, for as I ran I was running in Detroit, envisioning the city's parks and streets, avenues and expressways, with such eidetic clarity, I had only to transcribe them when I returned to our flat, re-creating Detroit in my novel *Do With Me What You Will* as faithfully as I'd re-created Detroit in *them,* when I was living there. What a curious experience! Without the bouts of running, I don't believe I could have written the novel; yet how perverse, one thinks, to be living in one of the world's most beautiful cities, London, and to be dreaming of one of the world's most problematic cities, Detroit.

Both running and writing are highly addictive activities; both are, for me, inextricably bound up with consciousness. I can't recall a time when I wasn't running, and I can't recall a time when I wasn't writing. (Before I could write what might be called human words in the English language, I eagerly emulated grown-ups' handwriting in pencil scribbles. My first "novels"—which, I'm afraid, my loving parents still have, in a trunk or a drawer on our old farm property in Millersport, New York—were tablets of inspired scribbles illustrated by line drawings of chickens, horses, and upright cats. For I had not yet mastered the trickier human form, as I was years from mastering human psychology.) My earliest outdoor memories have to do with the special solitude of running or hiking in our pear and apple orchards, through fields of wind-rustling corn towering over my head, along farmers' lanes and on bluffs above the Tonawanda Creek. Through childhood I hiked, roamed, tirelessly "explored" the countryside; neighboring farms, a treasure trove of old barns, abandoned houses and forbidden properties of all kinds, some of them presumably dangerous, like cisterns and wells covered with loose boards. These activities are intimately bound up with storytelling, for always there's a ghost-self, a "fictitious" self, in such settings. For this reason I believe that any form of art is a species of exploration and transgression. (I never saw a NO TRESPASSING sign that wasn't a summons to my rebellious blood. Such signs, dutifully posted on trees and fence railings, might as well cry COME RIGHT IN!) To write is to invade another's space, if only to memorialize it; to write is to invite angry censure from those who don't write, or who don't write in quite the way you do, for whom you may seem a threat. Art by its nature is a transgressive act, and artists must accept being punished for it. The more original and unsettling their art, the more devastating the punishment.

If writing involves punishment, at least for some of us, the act of running even in adulthood can evoke painful memories of having been, long ago, as children, chased by tormentors. (Is there any adult who hasn't such memories? Are there any adult women who have not been, in one way or another, sexually molested or threatened?) That adrenaline rush like an injection to the heart! I attended a one-room country schoolhouse in which eight very disparate grades were taught by a single overworked woman teacher; the teasing, pummeling, pinching, punching, mauling and kicking and verbal abuse that surrounded the relative sanctuary of the schoolhouse simply had to be endured, for in those days there were no protective laws against such mistreatment; this was a laissez-faire era in which a man might beat his wife and children, and police would rarely intervene except in cases of serious injuries or deaths. Often when I'm running in the most idyllic landscapes, I'm reminded of the panicked childhood running of decades ago; I was one of those luckless children without older brothers or sisters to protect her against the systematic cruelty of older classmates, thus fair game. I don't believe I was singled out (because my grades were high, for instance) and came to see years later that such abuse is generic, not personal; it must prevail through the species; it allows us insight into the experiences of others, a sense of what a more enduring panic, entrapment, suffering, and despair must be truly like. Sexual abuse seems to us the most repellent kind of abuse, and it's certainly the abuse that nourishes a palliative amnesia.

Beyond the lines of printed words in my books are the settings in which the books were imagined and without which the books could not exist. Sometime in 1985, for instance, running along the Delaware River south of Yardley, Pennsylvania, I glanced up and saw the ruins of a railroad bridge, and experienced in a flash such a vivid, visceral memory of crossing a footbridge beside a similar railroad trestle high above the Erie Canal, in Lockport, New York, when I was twelve to fourteen years old, that I saw the possibility of a novel; this would become *You Must Remember This*, set in a mythical upstate New York city very like the original. Yet often the reverse occurs: I find myself running in a place so intriguing to me, amid houses, or the backs of houses, so mysterious, I'm fated to write about these sights, to bring them to life (as it's said) in fiction. I'm a writer absolutely mesmerized by places; much of my writing is a way of assuaging homesickness, and the settings my characters inhabit are as crucial to me as the characters themselves. I couldn't write even a very short story without vividly "seeing" what its characters see.

Stories come to us as wraiths requiring precise embodiments. Running seems to allow me, ideally, an expanded consciousness in which I can envision what I'm writing as a film or a dream; I rarely invent at the typewriter, but recall what I've experienced; I don't use a word processor, but write in longhand, at considerable length. (Again, I know: Writers are crazy.) By the time I come to type out my writing formally I've envisioned it repeatedly. I've never thought of writing as the mere arrangement of words on the page but the attempted embodiment of a vision; a complex of emotions; raw experience. The effort of memorable art is to evoke in the reader or spectactor emotions appropriate to that effort. Running is a meditation; more practicably, it allows me to scroll through, in my mind's eye, the pages I've just written, proofreading for errors and improvements. My method is one of continuous revision; while writing a long novel, every day I loop back to earlier sections, to rewrite, in order to maintain a consistent, fluid voice; when I write the final two or three chapters of a novel, I write them simultaneously with the rewriting of the opening of the novel, so that, ideally at least, the novel is like a river uniformly flowing, each passage concurrent with all the others. Dreams may be temporary flights into madness that, by some law of neurophysiology unclear to us, keep us from actual madness; so too the twin activities of running/writing keep the writer reasonably sane, and with the hope, however illusory and temporary, of control.

"WHAT SIN TO ME UNKNOWN . . ."

All my life I've been fascinated with the mystery of human personality. Who are we?—so diverse, yet, perhaps, beneath diversity, so much akin? Why are we here? And where *is* here? The mystery of human existence shades into the mystery of physical matter itself and the questions that abide are those of the ancient philosophers: Why is there something and not instead nothing? What is the purpose of consciousness, and of human inquiry, itself?

When we begin as writers, of course, it's out of a fascination with language; with the mysterious sound, music, power of words. The sense of subterranean meanings beneath public discourse. The sense of the unpredictable, the playful, and the ungovernable; the inexpressible as it defines itself, through us, in language. As children, we acquire a talismanic power by imitating the speech of our elders; what begins as mimesis evolves into what we realize, one day, glancing about ourselves in wonder, is—what? Life itself? The most seemingly conscious of artists acknowledges his subordination to *discovery:*

> *. . . In fashioning a work of art we are by no means free, we do not choose how we shall make it but . . . it pre-exists us and therefore we are obliged, since it is both necessary and hidden, to do what we should have to do if it were a law of nature—that is to say, to discover it.*
>
> *(Marcel Proust)*

What begins in childlike wonder and curiosity becomes, with the passage of time, if we persist in our devotion (or delusion), a "calling"; a "profession." Almost without knowing what we do, we find ourselves in places we've never been, nor even anticipated. We come into contact with worlds, and with people, utterly foreign to us. In doing so, in turn, we become other people; we mature into those adults of the world we'd so admired, in our youth. If we are very fortunate, we participate in a mystical evolution of the human spirit itself; that "enlargement of sympathy" of which George Eliot and D. H. Lawrence spoke in such idealistic terms.

But what are the origins of the impulse Wallace Stevens calls the "motive for metaphor"?—the motive to record, transcribe, invent, speculate? The late William Stafford says in a poem,

So, the world happens twice—
once we see it as is;
second, it legends itself deep,
the way it is.

The crucial word here is "legends" with its suggestion of storytelling; a secondary creation over and above the existential experience of the world in which we find ourselves. To experience seems not quite enough for us, we want to know what we've experienced; we yearn to analyze it, debate it, even, at times, doubt and refute it. "There is an ancient feud between philosophy and poetry," Socrates is noted as stating, in Book X of Plato's *Republic,* but is perhaps a way of saying that there is a continuous dissatisfaction in mankind with things as they are said to be; a continuous yearning for the playfulness of the imagination.

I suggest several theories of the genesis of art:

1. Art originates in play—in improvisation, experiment, and fantasy; it remains forever, in its deepest instincts, playful and spontaneous, an exercise of the imagination analogous to the exercising of the physical body to no purpose other than ecstatic release.

2. Art is fueled by rebellion: the need, in some amounting to obsession, to resist what *is;* to defy one's elders, even to the

point of ostracism; to define oneself, and by extension one's generation, as new, novel, ungovernable. Virtually all artists begin as children or as adolescents; in adolescents, the need to break away from the past is as powerful as the drive to reproduce the species. "I have lived some thirty years on this planet," Henry David Thoreau says, with typical modesty, in the first chapter of *Walden*, "and I have yet to hear the first syllable of valuable or even earnest advice from my seniors. They have told me nothing, and probably cannot tell me anything. . . ." The unfairness, the very inaccuracy of such a declaration strikes the necessary chord of youthful revolt.

3. Art is a means of memorialization of the past; a recording of a rapidly vanishing world; a means of exorcising, at least temporarily, the ravages of homesickness. To speak of "what is past, or passing, or to come"—in the most meticulous language, thereby to assure its permanence; to honor those we've loved and learned from, and must outlive. The writer who most keenly evokes a landscape, a way of life, a gathering of people is likely to be one who has been exiled from his birthright. In time, even his (or her) rebellion shifts to a bittersweet sense of loss; even hurt, anger, chagrin become priceless emotions, bound up with the energies of youth.

4. The artist is born *damned*, and struggles through his (or her) life to achieve an ever-elusive redemption, by way of art; a sense of one's incompleteness or inadequacy fuels the instinct for ceaseless invention, as in an extension of the very

self's perimeters. The visual artist "makes art" that one can see, literally; this physical matter becomes part of the artist's identity. As the Puritans lived in dread of being damned by God, Whose grace they could not assume, still less call down upon themselves through prayer or good works, so the artist seems to cast about for a way of re-creating himself in aesthetic terms that are also spiritual terms. Like William Butler Yeats he "makes and unmakes" his soul. His art works may be subordinate to an idea or a vision; they may be said to constitute a single work, comprehensible, if then, only in retrospect.

In the beginning, for the child, there is only life, and consciousness; "play" is indistinguishable from both. No child, not even the prodigy Mozart, "plays" for professional purposes, nor even to define himself as talented, a worthy object of others' attention. Though uttered in somber adulthood, describing the genesis of *Waiting for Godot,* Samuel Beckett's offhand remark "It all came together between the hand and the page" is illuminating.

When I'm asked, as sometimes I am, when did I know I "wanted to be a writer," my reply is that I never "knew" I wanted to be a writer, or anything else; I'm not sure, in fact, that I "want" to be a writer, in such simplistic, abstract terms. A person who writes is not, in a sense, a "writer" but a person who writes; he (or she) can't be defined except in specific terms of texts. Elsewhere I've stated that "JCO" is not a person, nor even a personality, but a process that has resulted in a series of specific texts. What is perceived as product by others is process from the artist's perspective. My earliest, most vivid memories have to do not with any "self" (I think that young children must have very blurred, shifting images of themselves) but with drawing and coloring with crayons; inventing play worlds, or what might be called secondary worlds; or, as philosophers might term them, "counter-factual worlds."

Why?—to what purpose? No doubt child psychologists have speculated on the phenomenon of children's imaginations and the extraordinary energy invested in play, and surely it has to do with testing the perimeters of the self and of "reality," and, of course, imitating adult models. But the fact remains that it is a mysterious activity, exciting, fascinating, unpredictable. Like Lewis Carroll's heroine Alice, the child plunges willfully down the rabbit hole, or through the looking-glass, into another dimension. This "other dimension" is a counterworld into which only one individual has access: ". . . The artist needs only this: a special world to which he alone has the key" (André Gide). The counterworld both mirrors the "real" world and distorts it; in it, you both are, and are not, yourself . . . the most primary, if unacknowledged, fact of artistic creation.

Recall the thrilling openings of the Alice books! In John

Tenniel's famous drawings, their intricate shadings so evocative of the dream state, a partly dematerializing Alice is seen pushing through a drawing room mirror in *Through the Looking-Glass;* she reemerges in a world less tidy than the one she'd known, but far more interesting—for everything, here, is *alive.* Chess pieces have metamorphosed into kings, queens, knaves of singular ferocity; flowers not only speak, but debate with passion; "snapdragonflies," "rocking horseflies," "bread-and-butterflies," fawns tame as house pets, animal-human figures out of childhood mythology—all participate in Alice's adventure in this "curious" country that is England, yet marked off like a great chessboard.

> *"It's a huge game of chess that's being played—all over the world—if this* is *the world, you know. Oh, what fun it is! How I* wish *I was one of them! I wouldn't mind being a Pawn, if only I might join—though, of course, I should* like *to be a Queen best."*

Alice's excited enthusiasm is that of a child about to embark upon the adventure of life, beginning as a Pawn and ending (in theory, at least) as a Queen. Alice is an epic heroine with whom any child can identify; sometimes reckless, sometimes rather shy; at all times questing, inquisitive. "Curiouser and curiouser!" she exclaims. The world *is* curiouser and curiouser, the more we plunge into it. Lewis Carroll's counter-factual worlds shade into nightmare, informed by a subtle subtextual theme of Darwinian evolution—"survival of the fittest"—that takes its most graphic expression in the numerous instances of eating in the Alice books. (Eating is surely an infant's preoccupation, and it's said that "being eaten" is a dark fantasy of childhood.) The conclusion of *Through the Looking-Glass* suggests terror narrowly averted, as Alice wakes from a scene of impending disaster; about to be crowned Queen, as she'd wished at the outset of her adventure, she discovers, at the celebratory banquet, that "Something's going to happen!" How familiar, in its essence, the dream logic that stands expectation on its head, reverses anticipation to horror within an instant:

> *And then . . . all sorts of things happened in a moment. The candles all grew up to the ceiling. . . . As to the bottles, they each took a pair of plates, which they hastily fitted as wings, and so, with forks for legs, went fluttering about in all directions. . . .*
>
> *At this moment Alice heard a hoarse laugh at her side, and turned to see what was the matter with the White Queen, but, instead of the Queen, there was the leg of mutton sitting in a chair. "Here I am!" cried a voice from the soup tureen, and Alice turned again, just in time to see the Queen's broad, good-natured face*

grinning at her for a moment over the edge of the tureen, before she disappeared into the soup.

There was not a moment to be lost. Already several of the guests were lying down in the dishes, and the soup ladle was walking up toward Alice's chair. . . .

Alice can escape from, by waking from, the nightmare prospect of being eaten; the adventures through the looking-glass, like the adventures down the rabbit hole, involve intense emotion, but the child-heroine is never seriously in danger. One "plays" at adult life in such classic childhood fantasies but can revert back, virtually at will, to a waking world, one's parents' home, where all is safe and controlled.

Then there are those gifted, blessed or accursed children who are themselves, in childhood, geographers of the imagination. It is probably not a rarity, the child-fantasist who develops his or her imagination consistently, but it is rare that we know of it, at least in much detail. Consider the extended, ingeniously labyrinthine counterworlds of the Brontë children—Charlotte, Anne, Emily, and their ill-fated brother Branwell. These precocious children, motherless and isolated in a rural English parsonage, their household dominated by an eccentric father with a predilection for melodramatic violence—a soldier manqué who had ended up, unfortunately for him, a country parson—created by way of communal storytelling two fantasy lands: Gondal (the invention of Emily and Anne: a fictitious island in the Pacific bearing a distinct resemblance to rural Haworth) and Angria (the invention of Charlotte and Branwell: an imaginary African country conquered by the British). Many years later, Charlotte designated a gift of their father's of twelve wooden soldiers as "the origin of our plays"—ordinary toys that sparked the children's imaginations to such extraordinary heights.

The Brontë children confabulated plays, mimes, games, and serial adventure stories; eventually, tales of Gondal and Angria were recorded in "Little Magazines"—tiny books filled with italic handwriting meant to resemble print. These remarkably detailed chronicles of imaginary lands were not short-lived preoccupations of childhood, to be abandoned at puberty: Charlotte wrote her final Angrian story at the age of twenty-three, and Anne and Emily continued their Gondal saga until they were twenty-six and twenty-seven respectively. Under the pseudonym "Currer Bell," Charlotte Brontë published *Jane Eyre* in October 1847, when she was thirty-one years old; under the pseudonym "Ellis Bell," Emily Brontë published *Wuthering Heights* in December 1847, when she was twenty-nine. (Emily would die a year later.) Has the transformation of private loneliness and childhood isolation into enduring works of art ever been more triumphant than this? The memorialization of childhood fantasy reimagined as adult passion and "fate"?

No one has written more intimately of the writerly impulse than John Updike, in his autobiographical *Self-Consciousness,* which focuses upon a self's points of consciousness—the very points at which (by way of skin, breath, speech and its impediments, yearning for transcendence) a child-self becomes defined. In the chapter "Getting the Words Out," in which Updike examines his stuttering, he theorizes that his writing has its origin in relationship to breath. And language is visual, too: Updike's wooden ABC's were "alphabetical symbols stamped on blocks . . . [marking] the dawn of my consciousness." Updike's mother wanted passionately to be a writer herself, yet did not succeed while Updike was growing up; his memory of hearing her type hour after hour, shut away in a room to which he wasn't allowed entry: "The sound of her typing gave the house a secret, questing life unlike that of any of the other houses up and down Philadelphia Avenue" (Shillington, Pennsylvania, in the 1930s). The child John discovered to his astonishment and hurt that "in my mother's head there existed, evidently, a rival world that could not co-exist with the real world of which I was, I had felt, such a loved component." *Writing* was clearly an adult, even a secret, preoccupation; it presented itself initially to the child John as a matter of graphic symbols, the literal type of newsprint and the "marvel of reproduced imagery" of comic strips. Updike was mesmerized by the world of popular culture, including Walt Disney's cartoons and cartoon strips; he speaks of "dead pulped paper quickened into life by . . . Dick Tracy or Captain Easy or Alley Oop." A love of comic strips blossomed into a love of copying them onto blank paper and even onto plywood, setting them in rows on his bedroom shelf. Updike's verbal virtuousity, the painstaking craft of his prose, has its genesis in these early acts of devotion: "The very crudities and flecked imperfections of the [cartoon] process and the technical vocabulary of pen line and crosshatching and benday fascinated me, drew me deeply in, as perhaps a bacteriologist is drawn into the microscope and a linguist into the teeming niceties of a foreign grammar."

It is instructive to note, in passing, that the fantasies of childhood, whether self-invented or acquired by way of popular culture, parallel, in essence, the fantasies of the race. Not "realism" (a convention most people believe to be primary) but a kind of "surrealism" is the mode of storytelling that seems to have predated all others. Legends, fairy tales, ballads, the earliest of preserved drawings and other works of "primitive" art are not at all realistic but magical, with claims of divine or supernatural origin; of course, they are anonymous. As if, on so dreamlike a level of human consciousness, we are identical and the intrusive "individuality" of more modern times is not yet a problem. As beat and melody underlie the most formally intricate works of poetry, so romance underlies prose fiction, and is perhaps indistinguishable from it. All writers—all artists—may be classified as romantics, for the very act of creating, *and of caring passionately enough to create,* is a romantic gesture. What begins as child's play ends, not ironically so much as rather wonderfully, as a "vocation," a "calling," a "destiny"—even, above a certain income level, a "respectable profession." But the origins of the impulse remain tantalizingly mysterious, and we no more understand them, for all our exegesis and our science, than we understand our dreams.

As witty Alexander Pope has said, in *Epistle to Dr. Arbuthnot:*

Why did I write? what sin to me unknown
Dipt me in Ink, my Parents', or my own?
As yet a Child, nor yet a Fool to Fame,
*I lisp'd in Numbers, for the Numbers came.**

*By "numbers," Pope meant rhythm and rime.

NOTES ON FAILURE

To Whom the Mornings stand for Nights,
What must the Midnights—be!

—Emily Dickinson

If writing quickens one's sense of life, like falling in love, like being precariously in love, it is not because one has any confidence in achieving *success,* but because one is most painfully and constantly made aware of ***mortality:*** the persistent question being, Is this the work I fail to complete, is this the "posthumous" work that can only make an appeal to pity . . . ?

The practicing writer, the writer-at-work, the writer immersed in his or her project, is not an entity at all, let alone a person, but a curious mélange of wildly varying states of mind, clustered toward what might be called the darker end of the spectrum: indecision, frustration, pain, dismay, despair, remorse, impatience, outright failure. To be honored in midstream for one's labor would be ideal, but impossible; to be honored after the fact is always too late, for by then another project has been begun, another concatenation of indefinable states. Perhaps one must contend with vaguely warring personalities, in some sort of sequential arrangement?—perhaps premonitions of failure are but the soul's wise economy, in not risking hubris?—it cannot matter, for, in any case, the writer, however battered a veteran, can't have any real faith, any absolute faith, in his stamina (let alone his theoretical "gift") to get him through the ordeal of *creating*, to the plateau of *creation*. One is frequently asked whether the process becomes easier, with the passage of time, and the reply is obvious: *Nothing gets easier with the passage of time, not even the passing of time.*

The artist, perhaps more than most people, inhabits failure, degrees of failure and accommodation and compromise; but the terms of his failure are generally secret. It seems reasonable to believe that failure may be a truth, or at any rate a negotiable fact, while success is a temporary illusion of some intoxicating sort, a bubble soon to be pricked, a flower whose petals will quickly drop. If despair is—as I believe it to be—as absurd a state of the soul as euphoria, who can protest that it feels more substantial, more reliable, less out of scale with the human environment? When it was observed to T. S. Eliot that most critics are failed writers, Eliot replied: "But so are most writers."

Though most of us inhabit degrees of failure or the anticipation of it, very few persons are willing to acknowledge the fact, out of a vague but surely correct sense that it is not altogether American to do so. *Your standards are unreasonably high, you must be exaggerating, you must be of a naturally melancholy and saturnine temperament. . . .* From this pragmatic vantage point "success" itself is but a form of "failure," a compromise between what is desired and what is attained. One must be stoic, one must develop a sense of humor. And, after all, there is the example of William Faulkner, who considered himself a failed poet; Henry James returning to prose fiction after the conspicuous failure of his play-writing career; Ring Lardner writing his impeccable American prose because he despaired of writing sentimental popular songs; Hans Christian Andersen perfecting his fairy tales since he was clearly a failure in other genres—poetry, play writing, life. One has only to glance at *Chamber Music* to see why James Joyce specialized in prose.

Whoever battles with monsters had better see that it does not turn him into a monster. And if you gaze too long into an abyss—the abyss will gaze back into you. So Nietzsche cryptically warns us: and it is not implausible to surmise that he knew, so far as his own battles, his own monsters, and his own imminent abyss were concerned, much that lay before him:

though he could not have guessed its attendant ironies, or the ignoble shallowness of the abyss. Neither does he suggest an alternative.

The specter of failure haunts us less than the specter of failing—the process, the activity, the absorbing delusionary stratagems. The battle lost, in retrospect, is, after all, a battle necessarily lost to time: and, won or lost, it belongs to another person. But the battle in the process of being lost, each gesture, each pulse beat . . . This is the true abyss of dread, the unspeakable predicament. *To Whom the Mornings stand for Nights, / What must the Midnights—be!*

But how graceful, how extraordinary these pitiless lines, written by Emily Dickinson some four years earlier, in 1862:

The first Day's Night had come—
And grateful that a thing
So terrible—had been endured—
I told my Soul to sing—

She said her Strings were snapt—
Her bow—to Atoms blown—
And so to mend her—gave me work
Until another Morn—

And then—a Day as huge
As Yesterdays in pairs,

Unrolled its horror in my face—
Until it blocked my eyes—

My Brain—begun to laugh—
I mumbled—like a fool—
And tho' 'tis Years ago—that Day—
My Brain keeps giggling—still.

And Something's odd—within—
That person that I was—
And this One—do not feel the same—
Could it be Madness—this?

Here the poet communicates, in the most succinct and compelling imagery, the phenomenon of the ceaseless process of *creating:* the instruction by what one might call the ego that the Soul "sing," despite the nightmare of "Yesterdays in pairs"—the valiant effort of keeping language, forging language, though the conviction is overwhelming that "the person that I was— / And this One—do not feel the same." (For how, a scant poem later, *can* they be the same?) And again, in the same year:

The Brain, within its Groove
Runs evenly—and true—
But let a Splinter swerve—
'Twere easier for You—

To put a Current back—
When Floods have slit the Hills—
And scooped a Turnpike for Themselves—
And trodden out the Mills—

The Flood that is the source of creativity, and the source of self-oblivion: sweeping away, among other things, the very Soul that would sing. And is it possible to forgive Joseph Conrad for saying, in the midst of his slough of despair while writing *Nostromo,* surely one of the prodigious feats of the imagination in our time, that writing is but the "conversion of nervous force" into language?—so profoundly bleak an utterance that it must be true. For, after all, as the busily productive Charles Gould remarks to his wife, a man must apply himself to *some* activity.

Even that self-proclaimed "teacher of athletes," that vehement rejector of "down-hearted doubters . . . / Frivolous, sullen, moping, angry, affected, dishearten'd, atheistical," that Bard of the American roadway who so wears us out with his yawp of barbaric optimism, and his ebullient energy, even the great Whitman himself confesses in "As I Ebb'd with the Ocean of Life," that things are often quite different, quite different indeed. When one is alone, walking at the edge of the ocean, at autumn, "held by this electric self out of the pride of which I utter poems"—

O baffled, balk'd, bent to the very earth,
Oppressed with myself that I have dared to open my
mouth,
Aware now that amid all that blab whose echoes recoil
upon me I have not once had the least idea who or what
I am,
But that before all my arrogant poems the real Me stands
yet untouch'd, untold, altogether unreach'd,
Withdrawn far, mocking me with self-congratulatory signs
and bows,
With peals of distant ironical laughter at every word I have
written,
Pointing in silence to these songs, and then to the sand
beneath.

Interesting to note that these lines were published in the same year, 1860, as such tirelessly exuberant and more "Whitmanesque" poems as "For You O Democracy," "Myself and Mine" ("Myself and mine gymnastic ever, / To stand the cold or heat, to take good aim with a gun, to sail a / boat, to manage horses, to beget superb children"), and "I Hear America Singing." More subdued and more eloquent is the short poem, "A Clear Midnight," of 1881, which allows us to overhear the poet in his solitude, the poet no longer in the blaze of noon on a public platform:

This is thy hour O Soul, thy free flight into the wordless,
Away from books, away from art, the day erased, the lesson done,
Thee fully forth emerging, silent, gazing, pondering the themes thou lovest best,
Night, sleep, death and the stars.

One feels distinctly honored, to have the privilege of such moments: to venture around behind the tapestry, to see the threads in their untidy knots, the loose ends hanging frayed.

Why certain individuals appear to devote their lives to the phenomenon of interpreting experience in terms of structure, and of language, must remain a mystery. It is not an alternative to life, still less an escape from life, it *is* life: yet overlaid with a peculiar sort of luminosity, as if one were, and were not, fully inhabiting the present tense. Freud's supposition—which must have been his own secret compulsion, his sounding of his own depths—that the artist labors at his art to win fame, power, riches, and the love of women, hardly addresses itself to the fact that, such booty being won, the artist often intensifies his effort: and finds much of life, apart from that effort, unrewarding. Why, then, this instinct to interpret; to transpose flickering and transient thoughts into the relative permanence of language; to give oneself over to decades of obsessive labor, in the service of an elusive "transcendental" ideal, that, in any case, will surely be misunderstood or scarcely valued at all? Assuming that all art is metaphor, or metaphorical, what really *is* the motive for metaphor? Is there a motive? Or, in fact, metaphor? Can one say anything finally, with unqualified confidence, about any work of art—why it strikes a profound, irresistible, and occasionally life-altering response in some individuals, yet means very little to others? In this, the art of reading hardly differs from the art of writing, in that its most intense pleasures and pains must remain private, and cannot be communicated to others. Our secret affinities remain secret even to ourselves. . . . We fall in love with certain works of art, as we fall in love with certain individuals, for no very clear motive.

In 1955, in the final year of his life, as profusely honored as any writer in history, Thomas Mann wryly observed in a letter that he had always admired Hans Christian Andersen's fairy tale, "The Steadfast Tin Soldier." "Fundamentally," says Mann, "it is the symbol of my life." (And what is the "symbol" of Mann's life? Andersen's toy soldier is futilely in love with a pretty dancer, a paper cutout; his fate is to be cruelly, if casually, tossed into the fire by a child, and melted down to the shape "of a small tin heart.") Like most of Andersen's tales the story of the steadfast tin soldier is scarcely a children's story, though couched in the mock-simple language of childhood; and one can see why Thomas Mann felt such kinship with it, for it begins: "There were once five and twenty tin soldiers, all brothers, for they were the offspring of the same old tin spoon. Each man shouldered his gun, kept his eyes well to the front, and wore the smartest red and blue uniform imaginable. . . . All the soldiers were exactly alike with one exception, and he differed from the rest in having only one leg. For he was made last, and there was not quite enough tin left to finish him. However, he stood just as well on his one leg as the others did on two. In fact he was the very one who became famous."

Is the artist secretly in love with failure? one might ask. Is there something dangerous about "success," something finite and limited and, in a sense, historical: the passing over from *striving*, and *strife*, to *achievement*? One thinks again of Nietzsche, that most profound of psychologists, who tasted the poisonous euphoria of success, however brief, however unsatisfying: beware the danger in happiness! *Now everything I touch turns out to be wonderful. Now I love any fate that comes along. Who would like to be my fate?*

Yet it is perhaps not failure the writer loves, so much as the addictive nature of incompletion and risk. A work of art acquires, and then demands, its own singular "voice"; it insists upon its integrity; as Gide in his *Notebook* observed, the artist needs "a special world of which he alone has the key." That the fear of dying or becoming seriously ill in midstream is very real, cannot be doubted: and if there is an obvious contradiction here (one dreads completion; one dreads the possibility of a "posthumous" and therefore uncompleted work), that contradiction is very likely at the heart of the artistic enterprise. The writer carries himself as he would carry a precarious pyramid of eggs, because he is, in fact, a precarious pyramid of eggs, in danger of falling at any moment, and shattering on the floor in an ignoble mess. And he understands beforehand that no one, not even his most "sympathetic" fellow writers, will acknowledge his brilliant intentions, and see, for themselves, the great work he would surely have completed, had he lived.

An affinity for risk, danger, mystery, a certain derangement of the soul; a craving for distress, the pinching of the nerves, the not-yet-voiced; the predilection for insomnia; an impatience with past selves and past creations that must be hidden from one's admirers—why is the artist drawn to such extremes, why are we drawn along with him? Here, a forthright and passionate voice, from a source many would think unlikely:

There are few of us who have not sometimes wakened before dawn, either after one of those dreamless nights that make us almost enamoured of death, or one of those nights of horror and misshapen joy, when through the chambers of the brain sweep phantoms more terrible than reality itself, and instinct with that vivid life that lurks in all grotesques, and that lends to Gothic art its enduring vitality.... Veil after veil of thin dusky gauze is lifted, and by degrees the forms and colors of things are restored to them, and we watch the dawn remaking the world in its antique pattern. The wan mirrors get back their mimic life.... Nothing seems to us changed. Out of the unreal shadows of the night comes back the real life that we had known. We have to resume it where we had left off, and there steals over us a terrible sense of the necessity for the continuance of energy in the same wearisome round of stereotyped habits, or a wild longing, it may be, that our eyelids might open some morning upon a world that had been refashioned anew in the darkness... a world in which the past would have little or no place, or survive, at any rate, in no conscious form of obligation and regret.... It was the creation of such worlds as these that seemed to Dorian Gray to be the true object... of life.

That this unmistakably heartfelt observation should be bracketed, in Wilde's great novel, by chapters of near-numbing cleverness, and moralizing of a Bunyanesque nature, does not detract from its peculiar poignancy: for here, one feels, Wilde is speaking without artifice or posturing; and that Dorian Gray, freed for the moment from his somewhat mechanical role in the allegory Wilde has assembled, to explain himself to himself, has in fact acquired the transparency—the invisibility—of a mask of our own.

Will one fail is a question less apposite, finally, than *can one succeed?*—granted the psychic predicament, the addiction to a worldly skepticism that contrasts (perhaps comically) with the artist's private system of customs, habits, and superstitious routines that constitutes his "working life." (A study should really be done of artists' private systems, that cluster of stratagems, both voluntary and involuntary, that make daily life navigable. Here we would find, I think, a bizarre and ingenious assortment of Great Religions in embryo—a system of checks and balances, rewards, and taboos, fastidious as a work of art. *What is your work schedule,* one writer asks another, never *What are the great themes of your books?*—for the question is, of course, in code, and really implies *Are you perhaps crazier than I?—and will you elaborate?*)

How to attain a destination is always more intriguing (involving, as it does, both ingenuity and labor) than *what* the destination finally is. It has always been the tedious argument of moralists that artists appear to value their art above what is called "morality"; but is not the artist by definition an individual who has grown to care more about the interior dimensions of his art than about its public aspect, simply because—can this be doubted?—he spends all his waking hours, and many of his sleeping hours, in that landscape?

The curious blend of the visionary and the pragmatic that characterizes most novelists is exemplified by Joyce's attitude toward the various styles of *Ulysses,* those remarkable exuberant self-parodying voices: "From my point of view it hardly matters whether the technique is 'veracious' or not; it has served me as a bridge over which to march my eighteen episodes, and, once I have got my troops across, the opposing forces can, for all I care, blow the bridge sky-high." And though critics generally focus upon the ingenious relationship of *Ulysses* to the *Odyssey,* the classical structure was one Joyce chose with a certain degree of arbitrariness, as he might have chosen another—*Peer Gynt,* for instance; or *Faust.* That the writer labors to discover the secret of his work is perhaps the writer's most baffling predicament, about which he cannot easily speak: for he cannot write the fiction without becoming, beforehand, the person who *must* write that fiction: and he cannot be that person, without first subordinating himself to the process, the labor, of creating that fiction. . . . Which is why one becomes addicted to insomnia itself, to a perpetual sense of things about to fail, the pyramid of eggs about to tumble, the house of cards about to be blown away. Deadpan, Stanislaus Joyce noted in his diary, in 1907: "Jim says that . . . when he writes, his mind is as nearly normal as possible."

But my position, as elaborated, is, after all, only the reverse of the tapestry.

Let us reconsider. Isn't there, perhaps, a very literal advantage, now and then, to failure?—a way of turning even the most melancholy of experiences inside out, until they resemble experiences of *value,* of *growth,* of *profound significance?* That Henry James so spectacularly failed as a playwright had at least two consequences: it contributed to a nervous collapse; and it diverted him from a career for which he was unsuited (not because he had a too grandly "literary" and ambitious conception of the theater but because, in fact, his theatrical aspirations were so conventional, so trivial), thereby allowing him the spaciousness of relative failure. The public catastrophe of *Guy Domville* behind him, James wrote in his notebook: "I take up my *own* old pen again—the pen of all my old unforgettable efforts and sacred struggles. To myself—today—I need say no more. Large and full and high the future still opens. It is now indeed that I may do the work of my life. And I will." *What Maisie Knew, The Awkward Age, The Ambassadors, The Wings of the Dove, The Golden Bowl*—the work of James's life. Which success in the London theater would have supplanted, or would have made unnecessary.

Alice James, the younger sister of William and Henry, was born into a family in which, by Henry's admission, "girls seem scarcely to have had a chance." As her brilliant *Diary* acknowledges, Alice made a career of various kinds of failure:

the failure to become an adult; the failure to become a "woman" in conventional terms; the failure—which strikes us as magnificently stubborn—to survive. (When Alice discovered that she had cancer of the breast, at the age of forty-three, she wrote rhapsodically in her diary of her great good fortune: for now her long and questionable career of invalidism had its concrete, incontestable, deathly vindication.)

Alice lies on her couch forever. Alice, the "innocent" victim of fainting spells, convulsions, fits of hysteria, mysterious paralyzing pains, and such nineteenth-century female maladies as nervous hyperesthesia, spinal neurosis, cardiac complications, and rheumatic gout. Alice, the focus of a great deal of familial attention; yet the focus of no one's interest. Lying on her couch she does not matter in the public world, in the world of men, of history. She does not count; she *is* nothing. Yet the *Diary,* revealed to her brothers only after her death, exhibits a merciless eye, an unfailing accurate ear, a talent that rivals "Harry's" (that is, Henry's) for its astuteness, and far surpasses his for its satirical and sometimes cruel humor. Alice James's career-invalidism deprives her of everything; yet, paradoxically, of nothing. The triumph of the *Diary* is the triumph of a distinct literary voice, as valuable as the voice of Virginia Woolf's celebrated diaries.

> *I think if I get into the habit of writing a bit about what happens, or rather what doesn't happen, I may lose a lit-*

> *tle of the sense of loneliness and isolation which abides with me. . . . Scribbling my notes and reading [in order to clarify] the density and shape the formless mass within. Life seems inconceivably rich.*

Life seems inconceivably rich—the sudden exclamation of the writer, the artist, in defiance of external circumstances.

The invalid remains an invalid. She dies triumphantly young. When a nurse wished to commiserate with her about her predicament, Alice notes in her diary that destiny—any destiny—because it *is* destiny—is fascinating: thus pity is unnecessary. One is born not to suffer but to negotiate with suffering, to choose or invent forms to accommodate it.

Every commentator feels puritanically obliged to pass judgment on Alice. As if the *Diary* were not a document of literary worth; as if it doesn't surpass in literary and historical interest most of the publications of Alice's contemporaries, male or female. This "failure" to realize one's gifts may look like something very different from within. One must remember that, in the James family, "an interesting failure had more value than too-obvious success"—as it does to most observers.

In any case Alice James creates "Alice," a possibly fictitious person, a marvelous unforgettable voice. It is Alice who sinks unprotesting into death; it is Alice who says: "I shall proclaim that anyone who spends her life as an appendage to five cushions and three shawls is justified in committing the sloppiest kind of suicide at a moment's notice."

In Cyril Connolly's elegiac "war-book" *The Unquiet Grave: A Word Cycle by Palinurus,* the shadowy doomed figure of Palinurus broods upon the melancholic but strengthening wisdom of the ages, as a means of "contemplating" (never has the force of that word been more justified), and eventually rejecting, his own suicide. Palinurus, the legendary pilot of Aeneas, becomes for the thirty-nine-year-old Connolly an image of his own ambivalence, which might be called "neurotic" and self-destructive, unless one recalls the specific historical context in which the idiosyncratic "word cycle" was written, between the autumn of 1942 and the autumn of 1943, in London. *The Unquiet Grave* is a journal in perpetual metamorphosis; a lyric assemblage of epigrams, reflections, paradoxes, and descriptive passages; a commonplace book in which the masters of European literature from Horace and Virgil to Goethe, Schopenhauer, Flaubert, and beyond, are employed, as voices in Palinurus's meditation. In "Lemprière," Palinurus suffered a fate that, in abbreviated form, would appear to cry out for retribution, as well as pity:

> *Palinurus, a skillful pilot of the ship of Aeneas, fell into the sea in his sleep, was three days exposed to the tempests*

and waves of the sea, and at last came to the sea shore near Velia, where the cruel inhabitants of the place murdered him to obtain his clothes: his body was left unburied on the seashore.

Connolly's meditation upon the temptations of death takes the formal structure of an initiation, a descent into hell, a purification, a cure—for "the ghost of Palinurus must be appeased." Approaching forty, Connolly prepares to "heave his carcass of vanity, boredom, guilt and remorse into another decade." His marriage has failed; the France he has loved is cut off from him, as a consequence of the war; it may well be that the world as he has known it will not endure. He considers the rewards of opium-smoking, he broods upon the recent suicides of four friends, he surrenders his lost Eden and accommodates himself to a changed but evidently enduring world. The word cycle ends with an understated defense of the virtues of happiness, by way of a close analysis of Palinurus's complicity in his fate.

As a myth . . . with a valuable psychological interpretation, Palinurus clearly stands for a certain will-to-failure or repugnance-to-success, a desire to give up at the last moment, an urge toward loneliness, isolation, and obscurity. Palinurus, in spite of his great ability and his conspicuous public position, deserted his post in the moment of victory and opted for the unknown shore.

Connolly rejects his own predilection for failure and self-willed death only by this systematic immersion in "Palinurus's" desire for the unknown shore: *The Unquiet Grave* achieves its success as a unique work by way of its sympathy with failure.

Early failure, "success" in being published of so minimal a nature it might be termed failure, repeated frustrations, may have made James Joyce possible: these factors did not, at any rate, humble him.

Consider the example of his first attempt at a novel, *Stephen Hero,* a fragmented work that reads precisely like a "first novel"—ambitious, youthful, flawed with the energies and naïve insights of youth, altogether conventional in outline and style, but, one would say, "promising." (Though conspicuously less promising than D. H. Lawrence's first novel, *The White Peacock.*) Had Joyce found himself in a position to publish *Stephen Hero,* had his other publishing experiences been less disheartening, he would have used the material that constitutes *A Portrait of the Artist as a Young Man;* and that great novel would not have been written. As things evolved, Joyce retreated, and allowed himself ten years to write a masterpiece: and so he rewrote *Stephen Hero* totally, using the first draft as raw material upon which language makes a gloss. *Stephen Hero* presents characters and ideas, tells a story: *A Portrait of the Artist* is about language, *is* language, a portrait-in-progress of the creator, as he discovers the range and depth of his genius. The "soul in gestation" of Stephen Dedalus gains its individuality and its defiant strength as the novel proceeds; at the novel's conclusion it has even gained a kind of autonomy, wresting from the author a *first-person* voice, supplanting the novel's strategy of narration with Stephen's own journal. Out of unexceptional and perhaps even banal material Joyce created one of the most original works in our language. If the publication of *Dubliners* had been less catastrophic, however, and a clamor had arisen for the first novel by this "promising" young Irishman, one might imagine a version of *Stephen Hero* published the following year: for, if the verse of *Chamber Music* (Joyce's first book) is any measure, Joyce was surely not a competent critic of his own work at this time; and, in any case, as always, he needed money. If *Stephen Hero* had been published, *Portrait* could not have been written; without *Portrait,* its conclusion in particular, it is difficult to imagine the genesis of *Ulysses* . . . So one speculates; so it seems likely, in retrospect. But James Joyce was protected by the unpopularity of his work. He enjoyed, as his brother Stanislaus observed, "that inflexibility firmly rooted in failure."

The possibilities are countless. Can one imagine a D. H. Lawrence whose great novel *The Rainbow* had enjoyed a routine popular fate, instead of arousing the most extraordinary sort of vituperation ("There is no form of viciousness, of suggestiveness, that is not reflected in these pages," said a reviewer for one publication; the novel, said another reviewer, "had no right to exist"); how then could *Women in Love,* fueled by Lawrence's rage and loathing, have been written? And what of the evangelical *Lady Chatterly's Lover,* in its several versions? In an alternative universe there is a William Faulkner whose poetry (variously, and ineptly, modeled on Swinburne, Eliot, and others) was "successful"; there is a Faulkner whose early, derivative novels gained him a substantial public and commercial success—imitation Hemingway in *Soldiers Pay,* imitation Huxley in *Mosquitoes*—with the consequence that Faulkner's own voice might never have developed. (For when Faulkner needed money—and he always needed money—he wrote as rapidly and as pragmatically as possible.) That his great, idiosyncratic, difficult novels *(The Sound and the Fury, As I Lay Dying, Light in August, Absalom, Absalom!)* held so little commercial promise allowed him the freedom, the spaciousness, one might even say the privacy, to experiment with language as radically as he wished: for it is the "inflexibility" of which Stanislaus Joyce spoke that genius most requires.

But the genius cannot know that he is a genius—not really: he has hopes, he has premonitions, he suffers raging paranoid doubts, but he can have, in the end, only himself for measurement. Success is distant and illusory, failure one's loyal companion, one's stimulus for imagining that the next book will be better, for, otherwise, why write? The impulse can be made to sound theoretical, and even philosophical, but it is, no doubt, as physical as our blood and marrow. *This insatiable desire to write something before I die, this ravaging sense of the shortness and feverishness of life, make me cling . . . to my one anchor*—so Virginia Woolf, in her diary, speaks for us all.

INSPIRATION!

Yes, it exists. Somehow.

To be *inspired:* we know what it means, even how it sometimes feels, but what is it, exactly? Filled suddenly and often helplessly with renewed life and energy, a sense of excitement that can barely be contained; but why some things—a word, a glance, a scene glimpsed from a window, a random memory, a fragrance, a conversational anecdote, a fragment of music, or of a dream—have the power to stimulate us to intense creativity while most others do not, we are unable to say. We all know what it was like to have been inspired, in the past; yet we can't have faith that we will be inspired in the future. Most writers apply themselves doggedly to their work, hoping that inspiration will return. It can be like striking a damp match again, again, again: hoping a small flame will leap out, before the match breaks.

I think the early Surrealists were surely right: the world is a "forest of signs" for us to interpret. The visual world contains "messages" beneath its apparent disorder, just as meanings lie beneath the apparent disorder of the dream. Images abound to those who look with reverence, and are primed to *see:* like the Surrealist photographer Man Ray wandering Parisian streets with his camera, anticipating nothing, but leaving himself open to document *disponibilité*; or availability; or chance. Surrealism's most haunting images were, at the outset, purely ordinary images, decontextualized and made strange—as the poet Lautréamont said, "Beautiful as the chance encounter of a sewing machine and an umbrella on a dissection table."

Unexpectedly open to *disponibilité* as any Surrealist was Henry James, who listened avidly to dinner table conversations in London social circles. (For years the popular novelist, whom we are quite mistaken to assume to have been introverted and bookish, dined out as many as two hundred times *in a single season.*) James was one of those who knew how to keep still, and to listen; he heard, or overheard, numberless gossipy tales; yet seized for the purposes of his highly wrought, abstruse and intensely personal art only a few, among them *The Aspern Papers, The Spoils of Poynton, The Sacred Fount*, and that masterpiece of fin de siècle psychological horror, *The Turn of the Screw*. (Having heard only about half of the riveting anecdote that would provide the comical plot of *Spoils,* James asked not to be told the rest: he didn't want his imagination contaminated by mere factual truth.) In revisiting Washington Square after years of absence from the United States, James claimed to have "seen" the ghost of his unlived American self—and wrote that remarkable ghost story, "The Jolly Corner," in which the unlived self, the other James, is both realized and exorcized. After the violent Dublin insurrection of Easter 1916, William Butler Yeats was indignant with the Irish rebels for sacrificing their lives, needlessly, he thought; yet for days he was haunted by a single mysterious line of poetry—a line repeating itself again and again—until finally his great poem "Easter 1916" organized itself around that line: "A terrible beauty is born."

I write it out in verse—
MacDonagh and MacBride
And Connolly and Pearse
Now and in time to be,
Wherever green is worn,
Are changed, changed utterly:
A terrible beauty is born.

Karen Blixen, writing under the carefully chosen pseudonym "Isak Dinesen," transmogrified personal experience, a good deal of it bitter, into apparently distant, if not mythical images; yet the biographical element in her work is consistent if one knows how to decipher the clues. For instance, in a late parable, "The Cardinal's Third Tale," of *Last Tales,* a proud virgin contracts syphilis by kissing the foot of Saint Peter's statue in the Vatican after a young Roman worker has kissed it before her—a detail that aroused a good deal of negative criticism for its apparent "frivolity" since, at the time of the book's publication, the secret of Dinesen's own syphilis, also "innocently" contracted, was not generally known. Young Jean-Paul Sartre was so profoundly struck by the hallucinogen-induced vision of a tree's roots that *La Nausée,* his first novel, virtually shaped itself around the hieratic image; an image that has consequently come to represent, however misleadingly, the Existentialist preoccupation with things in their mysterious and usually malevolent *thingness.*

In 1963 the poet Randall Jarrell received a box of letters from his mother, including letters he himself had written at the age of twelve in the 1920s; he immediately embarked upon what was to be his last period of creativity—virtually plucking poems, his wife has said, from the air. The title of the book says it all: *The Lost World.* Before this, Jarrell had been inactive; after this, he sank into depression. He died in 1965. The poet Theodore Weiss, having written a twenty-line poem, was inspired to work on it in subsequent days—and months—and, finally, years: twenty years altogether. Each line of the poem mysteriously "opened out into a scenario," shaping itself finally into Weiss's first book-length poem, *Gunsight.* Eudora Welty was moved to write her early story "Petrified Man" by hearing, week after week, the most amazing things said in her local beauty parlor in Jackson, Mississippi—in this story the writer effaces herself completely and allows the voices to speak. While driving in the Adirondacks, E. L. Doctorow happened to see the sign "Loon Lake"—in which everything he felt about the mountains ("a palpably mysterious wilderness, a place full of dark secrets, history rotting in the forests") came to a point. And there suddenly was the genesis, the organizing force, for his novel *Loon Lake:* "a feeling for a place, an image or two."

For John Updike inspiration arrives, in a sense, as a "packet of material to be delivered." In 1957, revisiting the ruins of the old Shillington, Pennsylvania, poorhouse, a year or two after his grandfather's death, Updike found himself deeply moved by the sight: "Out of the hole where [the poorhouse] had been there came to me the desire to write a futuristic novel"—a highly personal work cast in the form of a parable of the future. So Updike's first novel *The Poorhouse Fair* was conceived, the very antithesis of the typical "autobiographical" first novel. Norman Mailer's first novel, *The Naked and the Dead,* was, by contrast, a wholly deliberate effort, "a sure result of all I had learned up to the age of twenty-five." Mailer's characters were conceived and put in file boxes long before they were ever on the page; he had accumulated hundreds of such cards before he began to write, by which time "the novel itself seemed merely the end of a long active assembly line." But Mailer's second novel, *Barbary Shore,* seemed to come out of nowhere: each morning he would write with no notion of how to continue, where he was going. Where *The Naked and the Dead* had been put together with all the solid agreeable effort of a young carpenter constructing a house, *Barbary Shore* "might as well have been dictated to me by a ghost in the middle of a forest." Similarly, *Why Are We in Vietnam?*, Mailer's *Huck Finn,* was written in a white heat of three ecstatic months, dictated in a sense by the protagonist's voice—"a highly improbable sixteen-year-old genius—I did not even know if he was black or white." Joseph Heller's novels typically begin with a first sentence that comes out of nowhere, independent of theme, setting, character, story. The opening line of *Catch-22*—"It was love at first sight. The first time———saw the chaplain he fell madly in love with him"—simply came to Heller for no reason, could not be explained, yet, within an hour and a half, Heller had worked out the novel in his mind: its unique tone, its tricky form, many of the characters. The genesis for *Something Happened* was the inexplicable sentence "In the office in which I work, there are four people of whom I am afraid. Each of these four people is afraid of five people." And though, a minute before, Heller knew nothing of the work that would absorb him for many years, he knew within an hour the beginning, middle, and ending of the work, and its dominant tone of anxiety.

Joan Didion began *Play It as It Lays* with no notion of "character" or "plot" or even "incident." She had only two pictures in her mind: one of empty white space; the other of a minor Hollywood actress being paged in the casino at the Riviera in Las Vegas. The vision of empty space suggested no story, but the vision of the actress did: "A young woman with long hair and a short white halter dress walks through the casino at the Riviera at one in the morning. She crosses the casino alone and picks up a house telephone. I watch her because I have heard her paged, and recognize her name: she is a minor actress I see around Los Angeles but have never met. I know nothing about her. Who is paging her? Why is she here to be paged? How exactly did she come to this? It was precisely this moment in Las Vegas that made *Play It as It Lays* begin to tell itself to me."

In his *Paris Review* interview of 1976, John Cheever speaks of the way totally disparate facts came together for him, unbidden: "It isn't a question of saving up. It's a question of some sort of galvanic energy." The writing itself then becomes the difficult effort to get the "heft" right—getting the words to correspond to the vision. Surely one of the strangest of all literary conceptions is that of John Hawkes's *The Passion Artist*. In a preface to an excerpt from that novel in Hawkes's anthology *Humors of Blood and Skin*, Hawkes relates how, when he and his wife were spending a year in southern France, he found himself inexplicably unable to write, in the midst of a profound and paralyzing depression; "whenever I entered our house I thought I saw my father's coffin. . . . I had this vision even though both my parents were buried in Maine. Each morning I sat benumbed and mindless at a small table. Each morning Sophie left a fresh rose on my table, but even those talismans of love and encouragement did no good. All was hopeless, writing was out of the question." Then came an invitation for lunch. Hawkes was told a lively bit of gossip about a middle-aged man who went one day to pick up his young daughter at a school in Nice, only to discover accidentally from one of the child's classmates that the daughter was an active prostitute, already gone that day from the playground to a sexual assignation. Hawkes listened to the anecdote; saw himself walking toward a lone girl and some empty playground swings. . . . One or two further associations, seemingly disjointed, and he had the plot of what would be *The Passion Artist*. The paralysis had lifted.

The most admirable thing about the fantastic, André Breton said, is that the fantastic does not exist: everything is real.

In *A Portrait of the Artist as a Young Man*, Stephen Dedalus explains the Joycean concept of the "epiphany": "A sudden spiritual manifestation, whether in the vulgarity of speech or of gesture or in a memorable phase of the mind itself. He believed it was for the artist to record these epiphanies with extreme care, seeing that they themselves are the most delicate and evanescent of moments." That Joyce's concept of one of the most potent motives for art has become, by now, a critical commonplace, should not discourage us from examining it. In his own practice the young Joyce, in his late teens and a student at University College, Dublin, began to collect a notebook of "epiphanies" fueled by the ambition not only to write but to write works of genius. He collected approximately seventy epiphanies—sudden and unanticipated moments of "spiritual manifestation"—of which forty survive. Many were to be used with little or no change in *Stephen Hero* (Joyce's early uncompleted novel) and in *Portrait;* the stories of *Dubliners* are organized around such revelations, rather like prose poems fitted to a narrative structure. It might be said that *Ulysses* is a protracted celebration of epiphany fitted to a somewhat overdetermined intellectual (Jesuitical?) grid: a short story tirelessly inflated to encompass the cosmos. (In fact, *Ulysses* had its formal genesis in a story for *Dubliners* titled "Ulysses," or "Mr. Hunter's Day"—a story that, according to Joyce, never got beyond its title.) The epiphany has significance, of course, only in its evocation of an already existing (but undefined) interior state. It would be naïve to imagine that grace really falls upon us from without—one must be in spiritual readiness for any visitation.

Yet is the writer in truth the triumphant possessor of a secret world to which (in Gide's words) he alone has the key?—or is he perhaps possessed by that world? The unique power of the unconscious is that it leads us where it will and not where we might will to go. As dreams cannot be controlled, so the flowering of any work of art cannot be controlled except in its most minute aspects. When one finds the "voice" of a novel, the "voice" becomes hypnotic, ravishing, utterly inexplicable. From where does it come? Where does it go? As in any fairy tale or legend the magic key unlocks a door to a mysterious room—but does one dare enter? Suppose the door swings shut? Suppose one is locked in until the spell has lifted? But if the "spell" is a lifetime? But if the "spell" *is* the life?

So, the familiar notion of a "demonic" art: the reverse in a sense of Plato's claim for its divine origin—yet in another sense identical. Something *not us* inhabits us; something insists upon speaking through us. To be in the grip of a literary obsession is not so very different from being in the grip of any obsession—erotic love, for instance, in its most primary and powerful state. Here the object of emotion is fully human but the emotion has the force of something inhuman: primitive, almost impersonal, at times almost frightening. The very concept of the "brainstorm": a metaphor nearly literal in its suggestion of raging winds, rains, elemental forces. The extravagance of William Blake's visions, for example; the ecstasy of Kafka in writing his early stories—writing all night! tireless! enthralled!—no matter that he is in poor health and physically exhausted. "Odd how the creative power at once brings the whole universe to order," Virginia Woolf observes, 27 July 1934, but she might have gone on to observe that the "universe" is after all one's own very private and unexplored self: "demonic," "divine."

The genesis of Mary Shelley's *Frankenstein* is nearly as primitive as the appeal of that extraordinary work itself: after days of having failed to compose a ghost story (in response to Lord Byron's casual suggestion) Mary Wollstonecraft Godwin Shelley had a hypnagogic fantasy in her bed. "I saw the pale student of unhallowed arts kneeling beside the thing he had put together. I saw the hideous phantasm of a man stretched out, and then, on the working of some powerful engine, show signs of life. . . . His success would terrify the artist; he would rush away [hoping] this thing . . . would subside into dead matter. He sleeps; but he is awakened; he opens his eyes; behold the horrid thing stands at his bedside, opening his curtains." One of the central images of *Frankenstein* is that of a stroke of lightning that seems to issue magically in a dazzling "stream of fire" from a beautiful old oak, blasting it and destroying it: a potent image perhaps for the violence of the incursion from the unconscious that galvanized the author's imagination after a period of strain and frustration. (It cannot have been an accident that *Frankenstein,* telling of a monstrous birth, was written by a very young and yet-unmarried pregnant woman who had had two babies with her lover already, only one of whom had survived.) Following this waking dream of June 1816, Mary Shelley had her subject—spoke in fact of being "possessed" by it. So too the brilliantly realized vision of the monster comes to us with such uncanny force it is difficult to believe that it owes its genesis to so very personal an experience—and did not evolve from a collective myth. *Frankenstein; or, The Modern Prometheus* was published in 1818 to immediate acclaim; yet with the passage of years the novel itself has receded as an artwork while Frankenstein's monster—known simply and inaccurately as Frankenstein—has achieved dominance. The nightmare vision ends as it began, with a curious sort of impersonality.

Why the need, rising in some very nearly to the level of compulsion, to verify experience by way of language?—to scrupulously record and preserve the very passing of Time? "All poetry is positional," Nabokov notes in his autobiography *Speak, Memory;* "to try to express one's position in regard to the universe embraced by consciousness in an immemorial urge. The arms of consciousness reach out and grope, and the longer they are the better. Tentacles, not wings, are Apollo's natural members." For Nabokov as for many writers—one might say Boswell, Proust, Virginia Woolf, Flaubert; surely James Joyce—experience itself is not authentic until it has been transcribed by way of language: the writer puts his imprimatur upon his (historic) self by way of writing. He creates himself, imagines himself, sometimes—recall Walter Whitman changing his name to Walt Whitman, David Henry Thoreau changing his name to Henry David Thoreau—renames himself as one might name a fictitious character in a work of art. And the impulse can rise to the level of a sacred obligation, at least in a young author's ambition: "There is a certain resemblance between the mystery of the Mass," says James Joyce to his brother Stanislaus in a letter, "and what I am trying to do . . . to give people a kind of intellectual or spiritual pleasure by converting the bread of everyday life into something that has a permanent artistic life of its own . . . for their mental, moral, and spiritual uplift." (One is tempted to note here in passing that it was for their "mental, moral, and spiritual" preservation the citizens of Dublin suppressed Joyce's *Dubliners* and in effect drove him into his life's exile in Europe.)

No one has analyzed the complexities of a writer's life so painstakingly as Virginia Woolf in her many volumes of diaries and to a lesser extent in her correspondence. The slow evolution of an idea into consciousness; the difficult transcription of all that is inchoate, riddlesome; the sense of writing as a triumphant act; the necessity of surrendering to the unconscious (the "subconscious" as Woolf calls it, imagining it as "her");

the pleasure in language as sounds, beats, rhythms—Woolf writes so meticulously about these matters because she is trying to understand them. In a letter to Vita Sackville-West of 8 September 1928, she says:

> *I believe that the main thing in beginning a novel is to feel, not that you can write it, but that it exists on the far side of a gulf, which words can't cross: that it's to be pulled through only in a breathless anguish. Now when I sit down to write an article, I have a net of words which will come down on the idea certainly in an hour or so. But a novel . . . to be good should seem, before one writes it, something unwriteable; but only visible; so that for nine months one lives in despair, and only when one has forgotten what one meant, does the book seem tolerable.*

And of style:

> *Style is a very simple matter, it is all rhythm. Once you get that, you can't use the wrong words. . . . This is very profound, what rhythm is, and goes far deeper than words. A sight, an emotion, creates this wave in the mind, long before it makes words to fit it; and in writing . . . one has to recapture this, and set this working (which has nothing apparently to do with words) and*

then, as it breaks and tumbles in the mind, it makes words to fit in.

One thinks of the young Ernest Hemingway writing each morning in a Parisian café, groping his way into what would be his first book, *In Our Time:* writing at first with extreme slowness and difficulty until he set down his "one true sentence"—usually a brief declarative sentence—and could throw the earlier work away and begin his story. One thinks too of William Faulkner's composition of his greatest novel, *The Sound and the Fury,* which began as a troubling and inexplicable image—the vision of an unknown little girl with muddy underpants climbing a tree outside a window—and slowly expanded into a long story that required another story or section to amplify it, which in turn required another, which in turn required another, until finally Faulkner had four sections of a novel, published in 1929 as *The Sound and the Fury.* It was not until two decades later when Malcolm Cowley edited *The Portable Faulkner* that Faulkner added the Appendix that is now always published as an integral part of the novel.

"I am doing a novel which I have never grasped. . . . There I am at p. 145, and I've no notion what it's about. I hate it. Frieda says it's very good. But it's like a novel in a foreign language I don't know very well—I can only just make out what it is about." So D. H. Lawrence writes in a letter of

1913 in reference to his work-in-progress *The Sisters.* So vague and unformed was the young author's sense of his novel in its early "crude fermenting" he had intended it to be a potboiler of a kind: the novel that would eventually become *Women in Love*. He made several false starts in its composition before realizing that he must give his heroine some background: this background rapidly evolves into the germ of a new, separate novel about three generations of Brangwens—a social history of the English Midlands from before the industrial revolution to approximately 1913. In short, the "background" for the heroine of *The Sisters* became *The Rainbow,* published in 1915. (*Women in Love* was published in 1920: the two novels are radically different in structure, style, narrative voice, tone.)

Is it as a consequence of Lawrence's method of composition, or in defiance of it, that he published within a few years two of the great novels of the twentieth century, *The Rainbow* and *Women in Love?* Lawrence was the most intuitive of writers, yet he was willing to write numerous drafts of a work and even to throw away as many as one thousand pages, as he claims to have done with *The Rainbow.* His deep faith in himself allowed him the energy to experiment in following his voice and his characters where they would lead; temperamentally he was the antithesis of James Joyce, who imposed upon his work a purely intellectual scheme meant to raise it to the level of the symbolic and the archetypal. "Don't look for the development of [my] novel to follow the lines of certain characters," Lawrence says in a letter of 1919; "the characters fall into the form of some other rhythmic form, as when one draws a fiddle-bow across a fine tray delicately sanded, the sand takes lines unknown."

T*he sand takes lines unknown.* What more beautiful and precise image to suggest the very imprecision of the creative enterprise?—the conjunction between inner and outer forces we try in vain to understand and must hope in the end only to embody?

READING AS A WRITER:
The Artist as Craftsman

I.

And yet the only exciting life is the imaginary one.

—VIRGINIA WOOLF, *DIARY*, 21 APRIL 1928

Of course, writing is an art. And art springs from the depths of the human imagination and is likely to be, in the final analysis as at first glance, idiosyncratic, mysterious, and beyond easy interpretation. We think of that supreme artist of solitude, Emily Dickinson, in the ecstatic grip of inspiration—"Did you ever see a soul at the *white heat?*"—and we think of the youthful Franz Kafka in the throes of writing his first story, "A Judgment," working through the night to convert the "tremendous world I have in my head" into prose to release its pressure, he hopes, without "tearing me apart." We think, with less unqualified admiration, perhaps, of the youthful Jack Kerouac who didn't so much compose his memoirist novels as plunge head-on into them, typing compulsively through the night fueled by alcohol, Benzedrine, and mania to create what he called "spontaneous prose": *On the Road,* which made him both famous and notorious overnight, was written on a single taped-together sheet of Chinese art paper forming a prodigious 150-foot roll through Kerouac's manual typewriter. We think of Herman Melville's similarly ecstatic bouts of inspiration in the composition of his masterwork *Moby-Dick*, and we think of D. H. Lawrence's fluid, seemingly artless storytelling in such classics as "The Blind Man," "The Horse Dealer's Daughter," "The Rocking-Horse Winner," and *The Escaped Cock.* Without such rushes of feeling, private and untrammeled, there can't be creativity. And yet, inspiration and energy and even genius are rarely enough to make "art": for prose fiction is also a craft, and craft must be learned, whether by accident or design.

And here we arrive at a very different truth: that the writer, even the writer who will seem to readers and reviewers strikingly original, has probably based his or her prose style and "prose vision" upon significant predecessors. Consider the no-longer-young, unpublished poet Robert Frost studying with excruciating care the poems of Thomas Hardy, to the point at which the cadences of Hardy's language, if not the noble bleakness of Hardy's vision, would be so absorbed into Frost's soul as to become indistinguishable from it; with the astonishing result, which no one including Frost might have foretold, that Frost would one day become as great a poet as his predecessor, and far more widely read in the United States than Hardy has ever been. Consider the young Flannery O'Connor, drafting her first novella, to be titled *Wise Blood,* and discovering Sophocles' *Oedipus Rex* and Nathanael West's *Miss Lonelyhearts,* both of which made a profound, lasting impression upon her: Sophocles for the tragic dignity of Oedipus's self-blinding, which O'Connor replicates in *Wise Blood;* West for his acerbic style, his cruel genius for caricature, and his young male Miss Lonelyhearts as a Christ-fanatic in denial of his faith very like O'Connor's young Christ-fanatic Hazel Motes. O'Connor's indebtedness to Nathanael West is pervasive through her fiction, and even a mature work like "Everything That Rises Must Converge" retains the Westian turn of phrase, sharp, revealing yet funny; a comic tone abruptly turned savage in the story's concluding paragraphs.

Consider the young, exuberant Herman Melville so struck by his contemporary Nathaniel Hawthorne's collection of allegorical tales *Mosses from an Old Manse* that he revised his plans for *Moby-Dick,* shifting its comic-picaresque tone to a far graver, more elevated and tragic tone and creating in the process what is arguably the most powerful American novel of the nineteenth century, if not of the twentieth as well. Consider William Faulkner, a young writer in his mid-twenties casting about for a voice, a point of view, a vision, taking up and discarding such disparate models as Algernon Swinburne, Aldous Huxley, and even his contemporary Ernest Hemingway before discovering the more temperamentally kindred James Joyce, as well as Gustave Flaubert's *Madame Bovary* and Joseph Conrad's *The Nigger of the Narcissus,* masterpieces of consciously wrought prose that would have an incalculable influence upon Faulkner; as, in turn, Faulkner's idiosyncratic poetic prose would have an incalculable influence upon writers as diverse as Gabriel García Márquez and Cormac McCarthy. And there is Ernest Hemingway, generally credited with having transformed American prose by way of his minimalist, rigorously unsentimental vision, and yet immensely influenced by such distinguished predecessors as Mark Twain and Sherwood Anderson, without whose refinement of American vernacular, particularly in such masterpieces as *The Adventures of Huckleberry Finn* and *Winesburg, Ohio,* the famous Hemingway style might not have developed.

Sometimes, a writer of stylistic brilliance denies or is unaware of having been influenced by another writer, for as Virginia Woolf notes in her diary for 20 April 1935:

> *Do I instinctively keep my mind from analysing, which would impair its creativeness? I think there's something*

> *in that. The reception of living work is too coarse and partial if you're doing the same thing yourself.*

Here is Virginia Woolf mulling over the phenomenon of James Joyce's *Ulysses,* which she could not have failed to recognize not only as a work of astonishing genius but one that would alter the very concept of prose fiction irrevocably:

> *I should be reading* Ulysses, *and fabricating my case for and against. I have read 200 pages so far—not a third; and have been amused, stimulated, charmed, interested, by the first 2 or 3 chapters . . . ; and then puzzled, bored, irritated and disillusioned as by a queasy undergraduate scratching his pimples. And Tom [T. S. Eliot] thinks this on a par with* War and Peace*! An illiterate, underbred book it seems to me; the book of a self taught working man, and we all know how distressing they are, how egotistic, insistent, raw, striking, and ultimately nauseating.*
>
> (Diary, *16 August 1922)*

Woolf's protestation, which descends even to class snobbery, surely arises from simple jealousy, if not envy, for the energy and inventiveness of *Ulysses.* Here Woolf senses herself confronted by literary genius beyond her own; however grand her ambition for transforming English fiction, she could not have failed to register how anemic and "impressionistic" her own style is compared to Joyce's. Yet, in *To the Lighthouse*, *The Waves*, and most of all *Between the Acts*, Woolf will be clearly influenced by the revolutionary Joycean language so like music to the inner ear and elliptical in its communication of ephemeral states of mind in contrast to the nineteenth-century notion of "character."

Often, "influence" is not immediately discernible but may be said to suffuse a younger writer's sensibility, rather more in the way of character than in writerly terms. Anton Chekhov and Leo Tolstoy could not be more different as artists, and as visionaries, yet Chekhov revered Tolstoy as he did no other writer:

> *His illness frightened me and kept me in a state of tension. I dread Tolstoy's death. If he died, a large vacuum would be formed in my life. In the first place, I never loved any human being as much as I do him. I am an unbeliever, but of all faiths I regard his as the nearest to me and the one that suits me best. Second, when Tolstoy is part of literature, it is easy and agreeable to be a writer; even the knowledge that you have not accomplished and never will accomplish anything is not so terrible, for Tolstoy makes up for all of us. His activity justifies all the hopes and expectations that are pinned to letters . . .*
>
> *(Letter to M. O. Menshikov, 28 January 1900)*

Yet Chekhov continues in this letter to shrewdly criticize Tolstoy for the "too theological" *Resurrection,* only just published.

In the same way, though there is hardly a glimmering of the ever-subtle Jamesian sensibility in her prose fiction, Flannery O'Connor spoke of reading Henry James with enormous respect and attention. Ralph Ellison closely studied Ernest Hemingway and Gertrude Stein yet would seem to have learned far more, as a craftsman of sentences, from William Faulkner. The lyric fabulist Eudora Welty admired Anton Chekhov, the supreme realist; Henry David Thoreau with the eye of a visual artist for the rich details of the natural world, and a precise prose style to communicate that vision, loved the mythopoetic Homer and such religious-mystic works as the Vedic *Upanishad,* the most nonspecific, philosophical, and nonnaturalistic of texts. Richard Wright may have believed himself influenced by Dostoyevsky's *Crime and Punishment* while writing *Native Son,* but apart from the surface similarity of plot, there would seem to be little of the Russian's deeper, profoundly religious consciousness in this startling novel of black American ghetto life and racialism. We can understand to a degree why Henry James was fascinated by Honoré Balzac, not least by Balzac's great celebrity in the nineteenth century; yet Balzac as a stylist would seem to have had no effect upon James at all, and the melodrama of his characteristic plots is totally missing in James, where human relations of a subtle kind, and often merely interior revelations, constitute drama. (As when, in the quintessential James story, "The Beast in the Jungle," the middle-aged bachelor-protagonist finally realizes what most readers would have quickly discerned, that his is a life in which "nothing" has happened.) Yet, surprisingly, here is Henry James musing to himself in his notebook after having read a story by Sarah Orne Jewett, a minor contemporary of his whose best-known work is *Tales of New England:*

> *February 19, 1899*
>
> *Struck an hour ago by pretty little germ of small thing given out in 4 or 5 lines of charming volume of Miss Jewett . . . A girl on a visit to new-found old-fashioned (spinster-gentleman) relation, 'idealized her old cousin, I've no doubt; and her repression and rare words of approval, had a great fascination for a girl who had just been used to people who chattered and were upon most intimate terms with you directly and could forget you with equal ease.' That is all—but they brushed me, as I read, with a sense of a little—a very tiny—subject. Something like this. I think I see it—must see it—as a young man—a young man who goes to see, for the first*

time, a new-found old-fashioned (spinster-gentleman) cousin. . . .

Here follows a dense, and intense, paragraph in which James rapidly limns an outline for a story (to be titled "Flickerbridge," reprinted in *The Better Sort*) that clearly would not have been imagined, still less composed, without the inspiration of Sarah Orne Jewett's "The Tone of Time." Henry James's great notebooks, available in a single volume edited by his biographer Leon Edel and Lyall H. Powers, are highly recommended for young writers. This remarkable gathering of notes to himself by a writer of genius is filled with gems, revelations, and surprises, more obsessively detailed even than Virginia Woolf's diary.

I have my head, thank God, full of visions. One has never too many—one has never enough. Ah, just to let one's self go—at last: to surrender one's self to what through all the long years one has (quite heroically, I think) hoped for and waited for—the mere potential, and relative, increase of quantity *in the material act—act of application and production. One has prayed and hoped and waited, in a word, to be able to work* more. *And now, toward the end, it seems, within its limits, to have come. That is all I ask. Nothing else in the world.*

I bow down to Fate, equally in submission and in gratitude.

(14 February 1895)

The inspiration a writer takes from a predecessor is usually accidental, like the inspirations of our lives; those individuals met by chance who become integral to our destinies. We meet—we "fall in love"—we are transformed. (If not always permanently, memorably.) Obviously, a writer is most permeable to influence when he or she is young; adolescence is the fertile turbulent period, a time of luminous dreams and dream-visions when the examples of our elders loom large before us and would appear to be showing us pathways we, too, might take. As a young, already ambitious poet, Sylvia Plath, the perfectionist, typed out poems by such then-popular poets as Sara Teasdale, lamenting in her diary (1946), "What I wouldn't give to be able to write like this!" In her twenties, Plath was so determined to be a writer of saleable short stories that she coolly dissected the stories of the Irish Frank O'Connor: "I will imitate until I can feel I'm using what he can teach" (quoted in Ted Hughes, Introduction to *Johnny Panic and the Bible of Dreams,* by Sylvia Plath, 1979). Plath learned from writers as different as Wallace Stevens and James Thurber; she analyzed stories published in *Seventeen, The New Yorker,* and *The Ladies' Home Journal*; her diary is breathless with self-admonitions and pep talks:

First, pick your market: *Ladies' Home Journal* or *Discovery? Seventeen* or *Mlle?* Then pick a topic. Then think.

Send it off to *The Sat Eve Post:* start at the top. Try *McCall's, Ladies' Home Journal, Good Housekeeping* . . . before getting blue.

I want to hit *The New Yorker* in poetry and the *Ladies' Home Journal* in stories, so I must study the magazines the way I did *Seventeen.*

I will slave and slave until I break into those slicks.

(quoted in Jacqueline Rose,
The Haunting of Sylvia Plath, p. 170)

In the similarly frank, though not nearly so obsessive memoir *Self-Consciousness,* John Updike speaks of his country-bred childhood in which he was "in love with not writing but with print, the straight lines and serifs of it, the industrial polish and transcendence of it"; and of his early admiration for works as various as Eliot's "The Waste Land," Faulkner's *Requiem for a Nun,* the prose of James Joyce, Marcel Proust, and Henry Green. (Joyce, Proust, and Green glimmer yet in Updike's tessellated style, along with Vladimir Nabokov, a later discovery.) Yet in the much-anthologized, irresistible "A & P," Updike's most popular story, it's the voice of American vernacular—Mark Twain, Sherwood Anderson ("I Want to Know Why"), J. D. Salinger (*The Catcher in the Rye*) as predecessors—fitted to distinctly Updikean themes of class and sexual attraction.

John Gardner, another ambitious young writer even in adolescence, spoke of typing out works of exemplary fiction in order to "feel" the prose rhythms of another's language; Gardner was a particular admirer of Tolstoy, whose moralizing, didactic tone is echoed in Gardner's fiction. In D. H. Lawrence's *Studies in Classic American Literature,* Lawrence reproduces much of the prose of works he admires (Poe's "Ligeia" and "The Fall of the House of Usher," Hawthorne's *The Scarlet Letter,* Melville's *Moby-Dick*), commenting so minutely on the passages as to seem a kind of coauthor. This is an extraordinarily sympathetic, uncannily intimate criticism, in which Lawrence hotly discusses fictitious characters like Hawthorne's Hester Prynne as if they were, not mere constructs of language, but somehow *real:*

> *Unless a man believes in himself and his gods,* genuinely; *unless he fiercely obeys his own Holy Ghost; his woman will destroy him. Woman is the nemesis of doubting man. She can't help it.*
>
> *And with Hester, after Ligeia, woman becomes a nemesis to man. She bolsters him up from the outside, she*

destroys him from the inside. And he dies hating her, as Dimmesdale did . . .

Woman is a strange and rather terrible phenomenon, to man. When the subconscious soul of woman recoils from its creative union with man, it becomes a destructive force. It exerts . . . an invisible destructive influence. The woman [like Ligeia] is sending out waves of silent destruction of the faltering spirit in men. . . . She doesn't know it. She can't even help it. But she does it. The devil is in her. . . .

A woman can use her sex in sheer malevolence and poison, while she is behaving *as meek and good as gold.*

("Nathaniel Hawthorne and The Scarlet Letter*")*

Readers of Lawrence's similarly passionate fiction will recognize his narrative voice in such passages, in which textual "analysis" is taken to an extreme of identification and empathy. For Lawrence the moralist didn't believe that art is merely aesthetic or self-expressive, still less entertaining, but the primary vessel of truth:

Art-speech is the only truth. An artist is usually a damned liar, but his art, if it be art, will tell the truth of his day. And that is all that matters. Away with eternal truth. Truth lives from day to day. . . .

> *The artist usually sets out—or used to—to point a moral and adorn a tale. The tale, however, points the other way, as a rule. Two blankly opposing morals, the artist's and the tale's. Never trust the artist. Trust the tale. The proper function of a critic is to save the tale from the artist who created it.*
>
> *(Introduction, "The Spirit of Place")*

D. H. Lawrence is as intransigent, and controversial, a figure in our own time as he was in 1917–1918, the time of *Studies in Classic American Literature,* when he was involved in the composition of his most complex and ambitious novel, *Women in Love.*

An eager, eclectic reader in his youth, F. Scott Fitzgerald, who would become famous, and notorious, at an even younger age than Jack Kerouac, with the publication of *This Side of Paradise* (1920) when he was only twenty-four, was influenced to varying degrees by Joseph Conrad, Theodore Dreiser, T. S. Eliot, James Joyce, André Malraux, Ernest Hemingway, Booth Tarkington, Thomas Wolfe—and Gilbert and Sullivan; in his letters to his daughter Scottie, at the time a freshman at Vassar, he urges her particularly to read Daniel Defoe's *Moll Flanders,* Dickens's *Bleak House,* Dostoyevsky's *The Brothers Karamazov,* Henry James's *Daisy Miller,* Joseph Conrad's *Lord Jim,* and Dreiser's *Sister Car-*

rie—works of literary and cultural distinction Fitzgerald wished to emulate.

One of the most imitated short story writers of the past several decades, Raymond Carver, acknowledged his indebtedness to such precursors in the form as Chekhov, Isaac Babel, Frank O'Connor, V. S. Pritchett, and Ernest Hemingway; in *Fires: Essays, Poems and Stories* he notes in the Introduction that he has affixed to the wall beside his desk a fragment of a sentence from a Chekhov story: ". . . and suddenly everything became clear to him." Carver speaks of Lawrence Durrell and Henry Miller as writers he admired who had no obvious influence on his prose style, nor is there any immediately discernible Chekhovian influence in his writing, as there would seem to be, clearly, an echo of Hemingway in Carver's pared-back, minimalist prose with its emphasis upon dramatic dialogue; but the spiritual influence of Chekhov suffuses his later work, like the tenderly comic, anecdotal "Cathedral" with its subtle epiphany arising from a sighted man's identification with a blind man: "It was like nothing else in my life up to now." (The affinity with D. H. Lawrence's similarly tender, passionate story "The Blind Man" is evident here, too.) And Carver's last published story, "Errand," the most unusual work of fiction in Carver's career, is actually about Chekhov's final days and death, and an incident following his death, virtually transcribed from a biography of Chekhov but narrated in an urgent, poetically distilled style unlike Carver's characteristic conversational style; as if, approaching his own death (from lung cancer) at the young age of fifty, Raymond Carver had fashioned a new voice for this story of the premature death, at the age of forty-four (from tuberculosis) of his hero Chekhov. Carver's artistry in the short story comes to a culmination in such powerful stories as "Cathedral," "A Small Good Thing," "Feathers," and "Errand," as he had defined it in his Preface to the Franklin Library limited edition of *Where I'm Calling From:* the attempt to be "as subtle as a river current when very little else in my life was subtle."

In his homage to Nelson Algren, the novelist and filmmaker John Sayles remarks that "the people who influence you aren't necessarily who you're going to write like, but the fact of their existence, of the existence of their characters, the spirit in them, opens up a possibility in your mind." So too Nelson Algren greatly influenced Russell Banks by the strength of his personality. Cynthia Ozick succumbed to an early, near-fatal fascination for Henry James; a quirkily original stylist, Ozick has acknowledged what might be called moral or spiritual influences in predecessors as varied as Anthony Trollope and Isaac Babel, Edith Wharton and Virginia Woolf, Isaac Bashevis Singer and Saul Bellow, Bruno Schulz and Primo Levi, and her now nearly forgotten contemporary Alfred Chester. In adolescence Maxine Kumin was enthralled by W. H. Auden, and Nicholas Christopher by Dostoyevsky and John Donne.

Unlikely, or perhaps elliptical models are the norm: Maureen Howard pays tribute to Willa Cather whose fiction differs radically from her own; the experimental novelist Bradford Morrow pays tribute to Ralph Waldo Emerson, who wrote no fiction; the experimental/minimalist Black Mountain poet Robert Creely pays tribute to the New England poet Edwin Arlington Robinson, author of the popular "Miniver Cheevy," "Richard Cory," and "Mr. Flood's Party."

More logically, it would seem to us, Stephen King, one of the best-selling writers in American, if not world history, acknowledges a direct debt to his predecessor in Gothic horror/"weird" fiction, H. P. Lovecraft, who died nearly penniless after a desperate career publishing in pulp magazines without having seen a single hardcover collection of his stories. The postmodernist Gothic writer Joanna Scott acknowledges Poe as a significant predecessor. Another postmodernist, Paul West, acknowledges "the sound and fury" of Faulkner's seductively extravagant prose style; Rick Moody, the suburban milieu and "indirection" of John Cheever; Mona Simpson, the solitary heroism of Henry James; Quincy Troupe, the originality and "astonishing, American language" of Ralph Ellison. Peter Straub, one of a small number of literary writers who are also writers of genre, acknowledges an admiring kinship with Raymond Chandler, though Chandler was a pioneer of the genre called "hardboiled mystery/detective" and Straub is an experimentalist in "Gothic horror." (For a number of these acknowledgments, and others, see *Tributes: American Writers on American Writers: Conjunctions 29.*) Virtually all of these tributes derive from the young writer's impressionistic reading in adolescence.

Is there any moral to be drawn from this compendium, any general proposition? If so, it's a simple one: *Read widely, read enthusiastically, be guided by instinct and not design. For if you read, you need not become a writer; but if you hope to become a writer, you must read.*

II.

That is the mission of true art—to make us pause and look at a thing a second time.

—OSCAR WILDE

To the writer of fiction, reading fiction is a dramatic experience. It's often tense, provocative, disturbing, unpredictable. *Why this title? Why this opening scene, this opening paragraph, this opening sentence? Why this particular language? And why this pacing? And why this detail, or lack of detail? And this length, and this ending—why?* Because as fellow writers we realize we're not reading mere words, a "product"; we understand that we're reading the end result of another writer's effort, the sum total of his or her imaginative and editorial decisions, which may have been complex. We know, as perhaps ordinary readers, nonwriters, wouldn't care to know, that despite romantic notions of divine inspiration, no story writes itself; whatever the original inspiration, the story before us, whether a classic like Chekhov's "The Lady With the Dog" or Ernest Hemingway's "Hills Like White Elephants," or a story by an American contemporary like Cynthia Ozick's "The Shawl" or André Dubus's "A Father's Story" has been consciously, in some cases painstakingly *written.* It has been extricated, excavated, out of the privacy of the individual imagination and positioned in a communal space, on the printed page. Its interior, secret emotions, and associations for the writer mean nothing now. It has become an autonomous creation, in a sense a small vehicle of words that moves us through time, or in some cases fails to move us. *Why was this story written? Is this story significant enough to have warranted the effort first of its own composition, and secondly of the reader's participation? Is it original? Is it convincing? Is its language appropriate? Am I a slightly different person for having read it, than I'd been previously? Will I urge others to read this story, and will I want to reread it myself and to read other work by the author? Above all, what have I learned from this story—as a writer?*

Henry James spoke of the artist as, ideally, one upon whom nothing is lost. This is particularly true for the writer of prose fiction who must populate his or her imaginary worlds with "real" figures; and the worlds containing them must give the illusion of being "real" as well. What a writer *is* intellectually, morally, spiritually, emotionally will radiate through the work, like light on an overcast day in which there's no visible sun, so that all things appear illuminated equally. Yet we can change our characters, we can deepen our souls, certainly we can become more mature, more sensitive and observant through the discipline of writing, as photographers "see" more sharply through a camera lens, and one of the ways we can affect such change is by approaching the art of writing as a craft. In Annie Dillard's *The Writing Life* there's an illuminating exchange:

> *A well-known writer got collared by a university student who asked, "Do you think I could be a writer?"*
>
> *"Well," the writer said, "I don't know. . . . Do you like sentences?"*
>
> *The writer could see the student's amazement. Sentences? Do I like sentences? I am twenty years old and do I like sentences? If he had liked sentences, of course, he could begin, like a joyful painter I knew. I asked him how he came to be a painter. He said, "I liked the smell of the paint."*

"The Lady With the Dog": A Masterpiece of Chekhovian Art

. . . Every man had his real, most interesting life under the cover of secrecy and under the cover of night.

—ANTON CHEKHOV,
"THE LADY WITH THE DOG"

Composed in 1899, when Chekhov was thirty-nine years old, at the height of his literary powers yet in a meditative, melancholy phase of his life, this most famous story of Chekhov's may well have been fueled by the author's own memories of "secrecy" and the "cover of night." And its subtly elegiac tone, so powerfully evolving out of the passion of adulterous love, is surely a consequence of Chekhov's brooding upon his own steadily failing health. (He was dying by degrees of tuberculosis and had only four more years to live.) The sophisticated, cynical Gurov is a deft, elliptical portrait of Anton Chekhov in his dissatisfactions with himself as a man who felt estranged—"cold and uncommunicative" in the company of men—yet came alive in the company of women. As the prematurely aging Gurov comes passionately alive in the company of Anna Sergeyevna, who is half his age, provincial, and limited in education and experience:

> *Why did she love him so much? He always seemed to women different from what he was, and they loved in*

> *him not himself, but the man created by their imagination, whom they had been eagerly seeking all their lives; and afterwards, when they noticed their mistake, they loved him all the same. And not one of them had been happy with him. . . . And only now when his head was gray he had fallen properly, really in love—for the first time in his life.*
>
> *(translation by Constance Garnett, 1917)*

To know certain biographical facts of Chekhov's life isn't at all essential to an understanding of this story, but it's instructive to know that Chekhov was in fact borrowing heavily from his own life in composing it. For what we can make of our own experiences, including even our ambivalent feelings about ourselves, is as legitimate a subject as any for fiction.

First of all, the title: Chekhov's titles are direct and unpretentious, rarely "poetic" or didactic, yet significant nonetheless in symbolic or mythic terms. (So *The Three Sisters* and *The Cherry Orchard,* his greatest plays, have titles that are both literal and mythic in meaning: the "three sisters" suggests the three Fates, and the cherry orchard suggests the Garden of Eden.) "The Lady With the Dog"—frequently translated, "The Lady With the Pet Dog"—is obviously descriptive, and literal; yet it suggests an ironic juxtaposing of lady/woman/

female with "male": in this case the girlish, extremely feminine and religious Anna Sergeyevna who loves Gurov deeply and without restraint, though she perceives herself as an adulteress and a "low, bad woman," and the more experienced and jaded Gurov, a "dog" by contrast. Yet, Chekhov suggests, the lady is fated to love the dog, and the dog, the lady. This is their highly Chekhovian, which is to say bittersweet and irresolute fate.

A young writer, confronted with "The Lady With the Dog," is apt to miss its extraordinary ease of craft, for Chekhov isn't a self-regarding stylist in the mode of James Joyce, Marcel Proust, Vladimir Nabokov; his prose is luminous and translucent, never ornamental. In 1900, having just read "The Lady With the Dog," Chekhov's friend and fellow writer Maxim Gorky wrote to him excitedly, saying that Chekhov was "killing" Realism, for after Chekhov "no one can go further than you along its path, no one can write so simply about such simple things as you. After . . . your stories, everything else seems coarse" (quoted in *Chekhov,* by Henri Troyat, p. 239). Yet it isn't quite the case that Chekhov is "simple"—unless classic elegance is simple. The most accomplished art may be to disguise "art" altogether. Chekhov's language is direct and even conversational; never self-conscious or "poetic"; his use of metaphor is rare, and always precisely chosen. For instance, when Gurov is first beginning to fall in love with Anna, he compares her to other women with whom he has had affairs, including

> *very beautiful, cold women, on whose faces he had caught a glimpse of a rapacious expression—an obstinate desire to snatch from life more than it could give . . . and when Gurov grew cold to them their beauty excited his hatred, and the lace on their linen seemed to him like scales.*

"Like scales"—for these cold, rapacious women are like snakes. By contrast, the inexperienced Anna is imaged as " 'the woman who was a sinner' in an old-fashioned picture." Gurov is as much in love with his vision of Anna as with Anna herself; he's in love with his own fading youth, and with a nostalgia for a more moral, more profound "old-fashioned" past.

One of the distinctive features of a Chekhov story or play is its seemingly conversational tone. This "voice" is always intelligent and sometimes whimsical, playful, ironic; occasionally, as in "The Lady With the Dog," it becomes explicitly philosophical and analytical. Gurov's consciousness pervades the story even before we come to know him. There's an apparently impersonal, omniscient opening line:

> *It was said that a new person had appeared on the sea-front: a lady with a little dog.*

It was said is a modern analogue of *Once upon a time.* Immediately we're introduced to what is in fact Gurov's introduction to "a fair-haired young lady of medium height, wearing a beret; a white Pomeranian dog was running behind her." It's a graceful cinematic opening that brings us into the astute consciousness of Gurov, a man whom even "bitter" experience hasn't discouraged as a lover of women. Following a few necessary paragraphs of exposition, focussing upon Gurov's bourgeois background and character, we move into the first dramatized scene between Gurov and the young lady whom he's deliberately befriended. Part I is only three masterfully condensed pages; Part II, a little more than seven pages, brings us swiftly to the consummation of the love affair, its central dramatized scene in which Gurov confronts the remorse of Anna, which is unsettling to him, and the parting of the lovers which they believe to be final: "It's time for me to go north," thinks Gurov. "High time!"

Yet the adulterous love story which the principals believe to be over is not over. As in other Chekhovian works, seemingly casual actions have serious, protracted consequences. Gurov realizes that he has fallen in love with Anna; contrary to his sophisticated character, he makes a desperate trip to Anna's provincial hometown and with no warning confronts her at the opening night of an opera. This powerful scene is also cinematic: Chekhov notes the glamor and bustle of the opera house, establishing an ironic counterpoint to the intensely private and emotional experience the lovers are undergoing. Following this climactic scene, Part IV is a four-and-a-half-page coda spanning years in the lives of the lovers as they continue to meet surreptitiously. (What of their domestic lives? What of Anna's children? Only their love affair is highlighted, as in a play involving just two characters.) Few serious writers even attempt to write love stories of this sort, which are achingly realistic and yet skirt sentimentality and bathos, but Chekhov's art raises "The Lady With the Dog" to a kind of tragedy, as the irresolution at the conclusion of *The Three Sisters* suggests tragedy in the very banality of thwarted ideals. Gurov and Anna love each other, we're told, like "tender friends"; yet their anguish is such that they yearn to be "free from this intolerable bondage." Yet happiness for them is precisely that there's no evident solution to their predicament:

> *And it seemed as though in a little while the solution would be found, and then a new and splendid life would begin; and it was clear to both of them that they had still a long, long road before them, and that the most complicated and difficult part of it was only just beginning.*

"The Lady With the Dog" has the depth and breadth of a novella, like so many of Chekhov's stories. Where most short fiction focuses upon a brief time period, or may contain a single dramatized scene, this story takes its lovers through years of their lives and projects them into a speculative future. Throughout, Chekhov maintains a precisely orchestrated *background* to his dramatic *foreground:* first, we're in the idle summer resort of Yalta; then we're in Moscow, in winter, where Gurov's lyricism is confounded by a companion's banal comment on food ("You were right this evening: the sturgeon was a bit too strong!")—which may well be an ironic comment on erotic love; then we're at the opera house, and at last in a room in the Slaviansky Bazaar Hotel in Moscow, an impersonal setting for the lovers' passion. The story's secret core, so to speak, is this phenomenon of the intensely private, secret life lived in the very midst of a public, extraverted life; as Gurov thinks, in the epigraph above, most men live their true lives under "the cover of secrecy and of night":

> *All personal life rested upon secrecy, and possibly it was on that account that civilized man was so nervously anxious that personal privacy should be respected.*

The story's theme is like a bobbin upon which the thread of the narrative, or plot, is skillfully wound. Without the bobbin, the thread would fly loose. Lacking this thematic center of gravity, the story of "fated" lovers would be merely sentimental and unoriginal.

In general, fiction of a high quality possesses depth because it involves absorbing narratives and meritorious characters and is at the same time a kind of commentary upon itself. In Chekhov, among other writers of distinction, "fiction" is counterpointed by "commentary" in a delicate equilibrium. The commentary can be extricated from the fiction, as Ray Carver chose a succinct epiphany from Chekhov to affix to his wall: ". . . and suddenly everything became clear to him." But the fiction can't be extricated from the commentary, except at the risk of reducing it to a mere concatenation of events lacking a spiritual core.

"Hills Like White Elephants": Writerly Grace Under Pressure

> *I met a girl in Prunier . . . I knew she'd had an abortion. I went over and we talked, not about that but on the way home I thought of the story, skipped lunch, and spent that afternoon writing ("Hills Like White Elephants").*
>
> —ERNEST HEMINGWAY,
> *PARIS REVIEW* INTERVIEW

What felicitous use to have made of a single afternoon: skipping lunch, and composing a four-page masterpiece.

(In fact, according to biographer Kenneth S. Lynn, Hemingway spent several days on his honeymoon in 1927 revising an earlier draft of a story set in the Ebro Valley in northern Spain, which would evolve into "Hills Like White Elephants." But Hemingway's version makes a superior anecdote.)

Ernest Hemingway often spoke with admiration of "grace under pressure" as an ideal of character in literature and in life. His was a masculinized vision of strength fortified by will, and it's as readily applicable to the art of fiction itself: grace is what we might call fluidity, smoothness, "inevitability" of narration, and pressure is the need to keep the story as tightly crafted, as pared to its essentials, as possible. "Hills Like White Elephants" is a single-scene story, a very brief one-act play. In dramatic literature, the tauter the scene, the more emotionally effective; if the scene is protracted or repetitive and the audience gets ahead of the play, there's a slackening of attention; but if the scene is too short and underdeveloped, the dramatic experience will be thin, slight, sketchy, forgettable. The goal for the writer is to *fully realize* his or her material: to discover the ideal balance between fluidity of narration and background exposition, description, and amplification.

In a brilliant miniature like "Hills Like White Elephants," as in the kindred "A Very Short Story," Hemingway's goal is to move us swiftly and unerringly from Point A to Point B. There are only two characters, "the American and the girl with him" (whom contemporary writers would probably call a "woman" since she would seem to be over eighteen). We don't know the names of these characters because they are evoked purely for this fragment of a scene, a "he" and a "she" whose attitude toward the unnamed "thing" (presumably an abortion) is antithetical; we are not intended to imagine lives for these characters beyond the scene in the train station bar. Short as it is, "Hills Like White Elephants" achieves a startling and dramatic closure, as perfect a match of content and form as the dazzling sonnets of William Butler Yeats.

The young writer can instructively contrast "Hills Like White Elephants" with the more complex, more leisurely "The Lady With the Dog" and with other more developed Hemingway stories like the classics "The Snows of Kilimanjaro" and "The Short Happy Life of Francis Macomber" which are structured like compact novellas. It's possible to imagine alternative, fuller versions of this story, written by the author in a later and more meditative phase of his life (Hemingway was only twenty-eight when he wrote "Hills . . .") in which the past relations of the young woman and her callow companion have been explored with thematic reference to the present situation; these characters would have names, histories, personalities, and their experience might merge with our own. For longer fiction has the distinct advantage of involving the reader emotionally, while minimalist fiction has the advantage of short, sharp, declarative art: surprise and revelation.

Note how the scene is set in the first, precisely written paragraph: as in "The Lady With the Dog," we open with what might be called a quick cinematic "establishing" shot.

> *The hills across the valley of the Ebro were long and white. On this side there was no shade and no trees and the station was between two lines of rails in the sun.*

How subtly it's suggested subliminally that romance of a kind is in the distance, across a valley, while "on this side" there's no shade and it's "very hot" and the primary concern of travelers is "What should we drink?"

Rare in Hemingway, yet altogether convincing here, a woman—a "girl"—is the bearer of a visionary truth, as she is the potential bearer of a child whose father would like it aborted. She is the one of the two who has an eye for poetic metaphor: she observes that the distant hills resemble white elephants while her companion says flatly, "I've never seen one," and drinks his beer. The girl, who surely hasn't seen a white elephant either, responds with a taunt, "No, you wouldn't have." In this brief exchange, their personalities are effectively contrasted and a sense of their discord is established. The story reaches a pitch of understated emotion as the two discuss the possibility of an abortion without ever quite naming what the "awfully simple operation" is; the girl, gazing out across the river valley, responds in a rush of inspiration which her companion, concerned with his own welfare, tries to block:

> *"And we could have all this," she said. "And we could have everything and every day we make it more impossible."*
>
> *"What did you say?"*
>
> *"I said we could have everything."*
>
> *"We can have everything."*
>
> *"No, we can't."*
>
> *"We can have the whole world."*
>
> *"No, we can't."*
>
> *"We can go everywhere."*
>
> *"No, we can't. It isn't ours any more."*
>
> *"It's ours."*
>
> *"No, it isn't. And once they take it away, you never get it back."*

(Who is this mysterious "they" who can take the world from us? So Hemingway has elsewhere evoked a kind of impersonal, godless fate that lies in wait for individuals who violate an unstated moral code.)

Judging from this exchange, the reader can assume that the man and the girl have been debating this issue for some time, without resolution; that the girl will probably give in

("Then I'll do it. Because I don't care about me"); that their relationship, which they call love, won't endure the strain of the abortion and its emotional aftermath. Hemingway seems to be suggesting, oddly for one with his well-known antagonism for traditional religion and morals, that we provoke punishment when we "violate" nature and the natural laws of sexual reproduction; when we live purely for ourselves, like these deracinated American travelers of the 1920s in a post–World War I malaise of the spirit. What is notable about the story, apart from its powerful theme, is of course Hemingway's highly stylized, wonderfully honed language. In his time, now decades past, such blunt, direct speech and the recording, in prose, of "the way people really talk" (even if they don't in fact really talk this way but with far less art) had the force of a revolution in consciousness. And Hemingway's idealism shone through the flawed, often wounded actors of his imagination as challenge and guidance for us all:

> *From things that have happened and from all things that you know and all those you cannot know, you make something through your invention that is not a representation but a whole new thing truer than anything true and alive, and you make it alive, and if you make it well enough, you give it immortality. That is why you write and for no other reason. . . .*

(See *Writers at Work, The Paris Review* interviews edited by George Plimpton, 1963.)

The short stories discussed in this essay have been selected because they represent, in most cases, works of prose fiction that have transcended their immediate time and the occasion of their first publications. They represent, to the individual, and very diverse writers, solutions in prose to problems of aesthetic form. *I have to tell* is the writer's first thought; the second thought is *How do I tell it?* From our reading, we discover how various the solutions to these questions are; how stamped with an individual's personality. For it's at the juncture of private vision and the wish to create a communal, public vision that art and craft merge.

THE ENIGMATIC ART OF SELF-CRITICISM

Self-criticism, like self-administered brain surgery, is perhaps not a good idea. Can the "self" see the "self" with any objectivity? The harsh, repentant mood of the moment may cast its doubt back upon an entire lifetime of creativity, with cruel results: the first great poet in the English language, Chaucer, not only came to doubt the worth of his extraordinary work in later life, but, overcome by Christian repugnance for what he perceived as the sin of secular creation, repudiated it utterly. So too, the Jesuit Gerard Manley Hopkins, centuries later, who came by tortuous degrees to believe that his lushly sensuous, markedly rhythmic poetry was a violation of his priestly vows. Franz Kafka's self-criticism, always severe, seems to have developed gradually into a species of self-laceration analogous to the powerful images of his work—masochistic fantasies of punishment, mutilation, and erasure. It is hardly surprising that Kafka asked his friend Max Brod to destroy all his work, including the uncompleted novels *The Trial* and *The Castle*. (Very sensibly, since he had a clearer and more generous vision of Kafka than Kafka himself did, Brod refused to do so.)

In the long history of literary effort, what eccentric self-judgments! Despite our best intentions it's problematic that, apart from immediate, practical, technical revisions, the writer's attempt to detach himself from his work, let alone his "oeuvre," is doomed: knowing too much may be a way of knowing too little. Or, how can we expect to know more about ourselves than we know about anything else?

Consider: in the human eye no light energy can stimulate the retina at the exit of the optic tract: all human beings carry blind spots with them in their vision. Everywhere we look there are points of invisibility, it might be said; and, since they are invisible, they can't be seen even as absence. These are the legendary "motes" in the eye of the beholder. They have their analogue in memory, as amnesiac patches drifting like clouds through our brains. It's rare that we actively and consciously "forget"; most of the time we have simply forgotten, with no consciousness of having forgotten. In individuals, the phenomenon is called "denial"; in entire cultures and nations, it's usually called "history."

"Do you know how many years I have to be read?"—so Chekhov asked his friend Ivan Bunin, at a time when no other

Russian prose writer except Tolstoy was so highly praised as Chekhov. "Seven years." "Why seven?" asked Bunin. "Well, seven and a half." Thomas Hardy, author of *Tess of the D'Urbervilles* and *Jude the Obscure,* novels of surpassing beauty and originality, spoke slightingly of novel-writing as a mere profession, a "temporary" but economically "compulsory" interruption of a poetic career. And what deadly combination of egotism and humility seems to have afflicted Albert Camus soon after being awarded the Nobel Prize: as if the public celebration of a career constitutes a curse, in private life. (In *The Fall,* Camus's fictitious narrator speaks of being persecuted by a "ridiculous" apprehension: "One cannot die without having confessed all one's own lies . . . otherwise, be there one hidden untruth in a life, death would render it definitive . . . this absolute assassination of the truth gave me vertigo. . . .")

Just get the right syllable in the proper place was Jonathan Swift's admonition, the perfectionist's credo. Yet, this credo can be the writer's nightmare. The strain of trying always to write beautifully, brilliantly, with originality, with "exultant" force can be self-damning, paralyzing. There is both vanity and humility in the despair of a perfectionist like Joseph Conrad, miserable in the composition of his most ambitious novel *Nostromo:* "I go on as one would cycle over a precipice along a 14-inch plank. If I falter I am lost." In a paroxysm of loathing for his task, Conrad spoke of being reduced to near-imbecility; of feeling that his brain had turned to water; and of his conviction that, for him, writing was simply the "conversion of nervous force" into words. (Does *Nostromo* suggest such writerly strain? Unfortunately yes, overall.)

The psychological phenomenon of paralysis itself, however, can be given an ingenious theoretical twist; so that, in contemplating the difficulties of writing, one is also contemplating the universal human condition: passivity, indecision, and "impotence" then become subjects for art, as in Mallarmé, Baudelaire, T. S. Eliot, Samuel Beckett. That sense that life has played itself out, that language is inadequate to communicate the intransigent facts of the human condition. *Why go on? Yet: we go on!* Beckett made a career of dramatizing this pseudo-tragic ennui, in poetic shorthand: "Moments for nothing, now as always, time was never and time is over, reckoning close and story ending" *(Endgame)*.

For some writers, the natural doubts of the self are amplified by critics' negative assessments: if you want confirmation of your essential worthlessness, you can always find it, somewhere. John Updike has remarked that the writer comes to feel that good reviewers are being generous while the others have really found you out. Since 1965 it has remained a perennial mystery why the much-praised J. D. Salinger ceased publishing in mid-career, though Salinger has not, evidently, ceased writing; yet if one considers the jeering and dismissive tone of critical response to Salinger's last-published books, the writer's dignified withdrawal into silence is understandable.

(What a feeding frenzy for critics, when Salinger's work is posthumously published. . . .)

Then there is the bravado of the wounded-but-defiant: "When reviewers like something of mine, I grow suspicious" (Gore Vidal).

More commonly, writers often have a very blurred conception of how their work is perceived by others, and what their work actually *is.* Herman Melville, for instance, the author, as a young man, of the best-sellers *Typee* and *Omoo,* seemed to believe that he had written another best-seller, a bowl of "rural milk" for the ladies, in the static, tortuous, parodistic *Pierre: or, the Ambiguities* (a novel that comes close to strangling on its own self-loathing and was to prove as dismal an economic failure as *Moby-Dick,* the novel of Melville's that preceded it). Charles Dickens seems sincerely to have considered *Great Expectations* a comedy, boasting of the opening section as "exceedingly droll" and "foolish"—material that strikes most readers as horrific, tragic. Scott Fitzgerald was convinced that his flawed, conventionally rendered *Tender Is the Night* was not only a great novel, but far more experimental than James Joyce's *Ulysses.* William Faulkner was convinced that his wooden, lifeless *A Fable* was superior to his brilliantly original earlier novels *The Sound and the Fury, As I Lay Dying,* and *Absalom, Absalom!*

James Joyce believed, or wished to believe, that *Finnegans Wake,* on which he had labored for sixteen years, was not one of the most difficult, abstruse, and demanding novels in the English language, but a "simple" novel: "If anyone doesn't understand a passage, all he need do is read it aloud." (Then again, in a less inflated mood, Joyce confessed: "Perhaps it is insanity. One will be able to judge in a century." Joyce offered no rejoinder to his brother Stanislaus's judgment that *Finnegans Wake* is "unspeakably wearisome . . . the witless wandering of literature before its final extinction. I would not read a paragraph of it if I did not know you.")

No one was more uncertain about her work than Virginia Woolf, perhaps because she thought about it, analyzed it, so obsessively. In November 1936 when she went over the proofs of *The Years,* the novel that had given her the most difficulty of her career, she noted in her journal that she "read to the end of the first section in despair: stony but convinced despair. . . . This is happily so bad that there can be no question about it. I must carry the proofs, like a dead cat, to L., and tell him to burn them unread." But Leonard Woolf said he liked the book; thought it in fact "extraordinarily good." (Leonard is lying, but no matter: Virginia can't know.) She notes in her diary that perhaps she had exaggerated its badness. Then again, a few days later, she notes that it *is* bad. "Never write a long book again." But a few days later: "There is no need whatever in my opinion to be unhappy about *The*

Years. It seems to me to come off at the end. Anyhow, to be a taut, real, strenuous book. I just finished it and feel a little exalted." Later, she concedes that it might be a failure after all—but she is finished with it. The first reviews, however, are ecstatic; Woolf is declared a "first-rate novelist" and "great lyrical poet." Almost universally it is said that *The Years* is a "masterpiece." A day or two later Virginia notes:

> *How I interest myself! Quite set up and perky today with a mind brimming because I was so damnably depressed and smacked on the cheek by Edwin Muir in the* Listener *and Scott James in* Life and Letters *on Friday. They both gave me a smart snubbing: E.M. says* The Years *is dead and disappointing. So in effect did James. All the lights sank; my reed bent to the ground. Dead and disappointing—so I'm found out and that odious rice pudding of a book is what I thought it—a dank failure. No life in it. . . . Now this pain woke me at 4* A.M. *and I suffered acutely. . . . But [then] it lifted; there was a good review, of 4 lines, in the* Empire Review. *The best of my books: did that help? I don't think very much. But the delight . . . is quite real. One feels braced for some reason; amused; round, combative; more than by praise.*

(*The Years,* all improbably, rises to the top of the best-seller list in the United States, where it remains for four months.

And we consider it, today, one of Woolf's least successful experiments, curiously dull and soporific—"no life in it"—unlike her genuine masterpieces *To the Lighthouse, Mrs. Dalloway, The Waves,* through which life flows with the quicksilver subtlety of light in a Monet painting.)

Any number of distinguished writers have been drawn into the challenge of rewriting and "improving" early work: W. H. Auden, Marianne Moore, John Crowe Ransom immediately come to mind. The energies of youth having passed, the aging and, it sometimes seems, vindictive elder wants to set things right: prune, revise, recast, in line with the doubtful wisdom of experience. His fellow poet George Seferis particularly denounced Auden's tampering with "September 1, 1939" (in which the famous line "We must love one another or die" was altered to "We must love one another and die"—or in another version omitted altogether, along with the stanza that contained it), seeing such revision as "immoral" and "egotistical" since the poem had long passed out of Auden's exclusive possession. W. B. Yeats's lifelong obsession with revising—the "making," as he called it, "of my soul"—was, by contrast, nearly always justified; as was Henry James's, and what we know of Emily Dickinson's. (Dickinson even did numerous drafts of her seemingly tossed-off little letters.) In rewriting early work for his *Collected Poems,* D. H. Lawrence considerably improved it, perhaps because the faithful poems were so bad to begin with. (However, Lawrence was a shrewd enough critic of his own work to understand that "a young man is afraid of his demon and puts his hand over the demon's mouth sometimes and speaks for him. So I have tried to let the demon say his say, and to remove the passages where the young man intruded." Note to *Collected Poems,* 1928.)

Of the innocence of raw egotism there are many, one might say too many, examples: that most macho of celebrated American writers, Ernest Hemingway, boasted of having beaten Turgenev and de Maupassant in fantasized boxing/writing matches, and of having fought two draws with Stendhal—"I think I had an edge in the last one." John O'Hara, the contemporary of such masters of short fiction as Thomas Mann, William Faulkner, Willa Cather, Katherine Anne Porter, Eudora Welty, and Hemingway, frequently boasted that "no one writes short stories better than I do." Robert Frost, even as an elder, much-honored poet, found it difficult to sit in an audience and hear another poet read work, particularly if the work was being well received, and it was wittily said (by John Cheever) that the Russian poet Yevtushenko has an ego capable of "cracking crystal at a distance of twenty feet." Nabokov believed himself superior to, among others, Dostoyevski, Turgenev, Mann, Henry James, and George Orwell.

In *The Wild Duck,* Ibsen speaks of the "life-lie"—the necessary delusion that makes life possible, gives us hope. (Even if it's an unreasonable hope.) For some writers, the "life-lie" is essential: they must believe that they contain genius, or they can't write at all. There is nothing wrong with such a conviction, except if it collides too dramatically with actual life.

To have a reliable opinion about oneself, one must know the subject, and perhaps that isn't possible. We know how we feel about ourselves, but only from hour to hour; our moods change, like the intensity of light outside our windows. But *to feel* is not *to know;* and strong *feelings* will block *knowledge.* I seem to have virtually no opinion of myself. I only publish work that I believe to be the best I can do, and beyond that I can't judge. My life, to me, is transparent as a glass of water, and of no more interest. And my writing, which is far too various for me to contemplate, is an elusive matter, that will reside in the minds (or, as Auden more forcefully says, the guts) of others, to judge.

THE WRITER'S STUDIO*

It's a room much longer than it is wide, extending from the courtyard of our partly glass-walled house in suburban/rural Hopewell Township, New Jersey (approximately three miles from Princeton) into an area of pine trees, holly bushes, and Korean dogwood through which deer, singly, or does-with-fawns, or small herds, are always drifting. Like the rest of the house my study has a good deal of glass: my immediate study area, where my desk is located, is brightly lighted during the day by seven windows and a skylight.

All the desks of my life have faced windows and except for an overwrought two-year period in the late 1980s when I worked on a word processor, I have always spent most of my time staring out the window, noting what is there, daydream-

*One in a series originally published in *American Poetry Review* 2003.

ing, or brooding. Most of the so-called imaginative life is encompassed by these three activities that blend so seamlessly together, not unlike reading the dictionary, as I often do as well, entire mornings can slip by, in a blissful daze of preoccupation. It's bizarre to me that people think that I am "prolific" and that I must use every spare minute of my time when in fact, as my intimates have always known, I spend most of my time looking out the window. (I recommend it.)

"It's just a turn—and freedom, Matty!"

A niece of Emily Dickinson would recount how the poet one day took her upstairs to her bedroom in the Dickinson house in Amherst, Massachusetts and made a gesture as if locking herself in with her thumb and forefinger closed upon an imaginary key. *Just a turn. And freedom.*

So with us all, I think. The precious room-of-one's-own. The private place, the sanctuary. To rephrase a famous remark of Robert Frost, our private places are those that, when we seek entry, we are never turned away.

Oscar Wilde noted that no man is a hero to his valet. We might say that no man/woman is heroic/oracular in private.

Thank God! Our natural instinct is to reject the Oracle, not to revere it. Above all, not to believe it.

The public oracular pronouncements of the literary icon are nearly always embarrassing, hollow, and expedient. Such lofty phrases as *the role of the poet—the voice of the poet—the conscience of the poet*—ring especially unconvincing in the poet's own ear, in private. "Did I really say such things? Why? I must have been in public."

Speechifying is not poetry. Airing grandiose views is not literature. Theorizing is mostly self-aggrandizement. Advertising for the kind of thing that you, with your specific limitations, can do.

Still, we find ourselves making such pronouncements, sometimes. It seems to be a professional hazard to which the writer/poet becomes increasingly susceptible with age. In proportion to the elder's increasing deafness, he becomes more verbose, oracular.

In public, we become public figures. But in private, we "become" the individuals we are.

On my desk, where I can always see it, amid a flurry of other paper scraps bearing crucial bits of information and admonitions, is a handwritten reminder in fading red ink:

Anything that happens to me as a writer has been precipitated by an action of my own.

This is an irrefutable fact and it means that I have no one to blame except myself when things go badly for me. Not hostile reviewers and critics. No one!

I would wish to think that serious art is transgressive, upsetting and not consoling, and that the serious artist can't really expect not to be attacked, ridiculed, dismissed; when it comes, the artist has brought his punishment upon himself. But maybe this is just wishful thinking, I'm hoping to exonerate myself.

In my study, as in any private place, I have to concede: the more we are hurt, the more we seek solace in the imagination. Ironically, conversely, the more imaginative work we create in this solitude, and publish, the more likely we are to be hurt by critical and public reaction to it; and so, again, we retreat into the imagination—assuring that more hurt will ensue. A bizarre cycle. Yet it makes a kind of sense. *How do you write so much?* is a question frequently asked of me. Less frequently asked is *Why?*

Writing, for me, is primarily remembering. Which means that "writing" isn't specifically verbal for me, as it must be for most poets: it's as likely to be cinematic, dramatic, emotional, auditory, and shimmeringly unformed before it becomes actual language, transformed into words on a page. Editors are sometimes surprised that I entirely rewrite pieces that have been accepted for publication. Often I surprise myself, I exasperate and frustrate myself, by entirely rewriting chapters of novels that had seemed quite acceptable the previous day; and, on later occasions, rewriting these. For always I feel that I have new ideas, always there seem to me more felicitous ways of expressing what I want to say. So this study I have been speaking of with its windows, skylight, admonitory notes, and works of art on windowsills, walls, surfaces, is, in a way, incidental to the process of my writing.

Rarely do I invent at the typewriter (a Japanese-made Swintec 1000 with an approximate ten-page memory, printing capacity, storage for disks), and virtually never do I try to force anything into prose in this way. I need to imagine first, purely without language; and then remember. I spend much of my time away from the study, in fact. I spend much of my time in motion. Running (my favorite activity, in which my metabolism seems somehow "normal"), walking, bicycling. Driving a car (cruise control recommended) or being driven in one. In airports, on airplanes. So often, airports and airplanes! And in that twilight state between sleep and waking in the very early morning, before the rudely steep climb of the day's foothills and mountains. These are interludes when I try to think through what I am going to write at a later time; I try to envision scenes, to "hear" speech. At my desk I remember, though not merely. I am one of those writers who needs to know the ending of a work before she can begin with much confidence and energy. Of course the work will evolve, all imaginative work evolves in time, once its roots are established. But the ending must be there, in the unconscious at least, before there can be a strong beginning.

Still, I love my study. It's the place to which I return, with myriad daydreams, sketchy memories, scraps of paper. (Emily Dickinson, too, wrote on scraps of paper, folded and placed in the pockets of her apron. In the evening, in the freedom of her room, she took out these scraps to contemplate them.) At certain hours of the day the room is flooded with light and it is often warmer than other parts of the house, ideal for a rather icy-blooded individual. The other day a near-grown fawn approached a window to peer inside at me. I thought her expression was quizzical, bemused. *What on earth is that human being doing? What can she be taking so seriously? Not herself, surely? But what?*

BLONDE AMBITION: AN INTERVIEW WITH JOYCE CAROL OATES

by

Greg Johnson

Joyce Carol Oates is a novelist well known for tackling large, controversial, uniquely American subjects.

Her novel *them*, winner of the 1970 National Book Award, culminated in a depiction of the Detroit race riots of 1967; *Because It Is Bitter, and Because It Is My Heart* (1990) dramatized an interracial teenage romance; and the Pulitzer Prize–nominated *Black Water* (1992) offered a fictional rendition of the Chappaquiddick incident, from the viewpoint of the drowning young woman. Oates's short, grisly 1995 novel, *Zombie*, suggested by the Jeffrey Dahmer case, explored the psyche of a serial killer in all-too-convincing detail.

Now Oates has produced her longest novel to date, a 738-page epic based on the brief, dazzling life of Norma Jeane Baker, better known as Marilyn Monroe. From her home in Princeton, N.J., Oates clarified her aims and ambitions in writing *Blonde* (Ecco/HarperCollins, 2000), a novel perhaps destined to become the most controversial of her career.

What was the genesis of Blonde? *What prompted you to choose Marilyn Monroe as the focus of a novel?*

OATES: Some years ago I happened to see a photograph of the 17-year-old Norma Jeane Baker. With her longish dark curly hair, artificial flowers on her head, locket around her neck, she looked nothing like the iconic "Marilyn Monroe." I felt an immediate sense of something like recognition; this young, hopefully smiling girl, so very American, reminded me powerfully of girls of my childhood, some of them from broken homes. For days I felt an almost rapturous sense of excitement, that I might give life to this lost, lone girl, whom the iconic consumer-product "Marilyn Monroe" would soon overwhelm and obliterate. I saw her story as mythical, archetypal; it would end when she loses her baptismal name Norma Jeane, and takes on the studio name "Marilyn Monroe." She would also have to bleach her brown hair to platinum blonde, endure some facial surgery, and dress provocatively. I'd planned a 175-page novella, and the last line would have been "Marilyn Monroe." The mode of storytelling would have been fairytale-like, as poetic as I could make appropriate.

Obviously, you've produced a long novel, not a novella. What happened?

OATES: In the writing, characteristically, the "novella" acquired a deeper, more urgent, and epic life, and grew into a full-length novel. "What happened" is what usually happens in these cases. *Blonde* has several styles, but the predominant is that of psychological realism rather than the fairytale/surreal mode. The novel is a posthumous narration by the subject.

After I abandoned the novella form, I created an "epic" form to accommodate the complexities of the life. It was my intention to create a female portrait as emblematic of her time and place as Emma Bovary was of hers. (Of course, Norma Jeane is actually more complex, and certainly more admirable, than Emma Bovary.)

What led you to choose this unusual point of view, "a posthumous narration" by Norma Jeane herself?

OATES: This is a difficult question to answer. The voice, point of view, ironic perspective, mythic distance: this curious distancing effect is my approximation of how an individual might feel dreaming back over his or her own life at the very conclusion of that life, on the brink of extinction even as, as in a fairy tale, the individual life enters an abstract, communal "posterity." Norma Jeane dies, and "Marilyn Monroe," the role, the concoction, the artifice, would seem to endure.

At over 700 printed pages, this is your longest novel but your original manuscript was even longer—1,400 pages. Why did you cut the novel so substantially?

OATES: At 1,400 pages, the novel had to be cut, and some sections, surgically removed from the manuscript, will be published independently. They are all part of Norma Jeane's living, organic life. To me, the language of Norma Jeane is somehow "real."

Still, a novel of such a length is a problem. Rights have been sold, according to my agent, to "nearly all languages" except Japanese, where if the novel were to be translated it would grow again by between one-third and one-half in length. In German, for instance, it will be massive enough!

You wrote and extensively revised this huge novel in less than a year. It must have been an intense writing experience.

OATES: I think, looking back upon the experience, that it is one I would not wish to relive. In psychoanalytic terms—though we can't of course "analyze" ourselves—I believe I was trying to give life to Norma Jeane Baker, and to keep her living, in a very obsessive way, because she came to represent certain "life-elements" in my own experience and, I hope, in the life of America. A young girl, born into poverty, cast off by her father and eventually by her mother, who, as in a fairy tale, becomes an iconic "Fair Princess" and is posthumously celebrated as "The Sex Symbol of the 20th Century," making millions of dollars for other people—it's just too sad, too ironic.

Could you describe your writing process as this novel evolved?

OATES: With a novel of such length, it was necessary to keep the narrative voice consistent and fluid. I was continually going back and rewriting, and when I entered the last phase of about 200 pages, I began simultaneously to rewrite the novel from the first page to about page 300, to assure this consistency of voice. (Though the voice changes, too, as Norma Jeane ages.) Actually, I recommend this technique for all novelists, even with shorter work. It's akin to aerating soil, if you're a gardener.

Since the 1960s, a number of well-known writers—Capote, Vidal, Mailer, DeLillo, and others—have focused ambitious novels on famous, and sometimes infamous, historical figures. Do you consider Blonde *as falling into this tradition of the "nonfiction novel"?*

OATES: The line of descent, so to speak, may derive from John Dos Passos's *U.S.A.* with its lively, inventive portraits of "real people" mixed with fictional characters. Dos Passos's Henry Ford, for instance, is an obvious ancestor of E. L. Doctorow's emboldened portraits in *Ragtime*. Some of these are rather more playful/caricatured than serious portrayals of "real people."

So much of *Blonde* is obviously fiction, to call it "nonfiction" would be misleading. (I explain in my preface: if you want historical veracity, you must go to the biographies. Even while perhaps not 100% accurate, they are at least predicated upon literal truth, while the novel aspires to a spiritual/poetic truth.)

Were you concerned that the glare of Marilyn Monroe's celebrity and myth might divert attention from your artistic goals? What was the advantage to you, as a writer, of using the skeletal reality of her life, instead of creating a wholly fictional actress-character to dramatize the "spiritual/poetic truth" you sought?

OATES: I'd hoped to evoke a poetic, spiritual, "inner" truth by selecting incidents, images, representative figures from the life, and had absolutely no interest in a purely biographical or historic book. Prepublication responses and interviews so far have indicated quite sympathetic and intelligent readings of the novel. Of course, there will be others, but angry or dismissive reviews can happen to us regardless of what we write, whether purely fiction or fiction based upon history. The writer may as well pursue his or her vision, and not be distracted by how others will respond in their myriad and unpredictable ways.

You did considerable research into Monroe's life and into the art of acting. Did you come to see parallels between acting and writ-

ing? Did you develop a sense of kinship with Monroe as you wrote the novel?

OATES: Not "considerable research" compared to my biographer/scholar friends. Rather, I created an outline or skeleton of the "life," collated with the "life of the time." (*Blonde* is also a political novel, in part. The rise of Red Scare paranoia, the betrayals and back-stabbings in Hollywood; the assumptions of what we might call Cold War theology: we are God's nation, the Soviet Union belongs to Satan.) All of my longer novels are political, but not obtrusively so, I hope.

Theater/acting fascinate, as a phenomenon of human experience. Why do we wish to "believe" the actor in performance, why are we moved to true emotions in a context which we know is artificial? Since 1990 I've been involved quite actively in theater, and have come to greatly admire both directors and actors. Norma Jeane seems to have been a naturally gifted actress because, perhaps, she so lacked an inner core of identity. "I guess I never believed that I deserved to live. The way other people do. I needed to justify my life." These were (invented) words of Norma Jeane's I affixed to the wall beside my desk. How many of us, I wonder, feel exactly the same way!

What concerns did you have in dealing with living people—for example, Monroe's third husband, the playwright Arthur

Miller—in a fictional context? Did you contact or interview Miller, or anyone else who knew Monroe?

OATES: No, I didn't interview anyone about "Marilyn Monroe." It was not "Marilyn Monroe" about whom I wrote. Norma Jeane marries mythic individuals, not "historic" figures. Her husbands include the Ex-Athlete and the Playwright. (If I wanted to write about Joe DiMaggio and Arthur Miller, I would need to write about these complex men in a different mode. Though, in fact, the Playwright is presented from the inside, often. It's clear that I identify with the Playwright, and that he becomes, eventually, the voice of conscience in the latter part of the novel. But I certainly didn't read Arthur Miller's memoir or any interviews with him about "Monroe.")

Monroe's reputation as an actress remains controversial. What is your assessment of her achievement as an artist?

OATES: She was a naturally gifted, often uncanny actress. Her fellow actors began by condescending to her, but ended by feeling awe for her on-film presence; she "out-acted" most of them. In movies, as in art, it isn't what goes in, but what comes out, that matters. Your process of, for instance, acting, or writing, is not important; only what it leads you to matters. And the process, mysteriously, would seem to have little to do with that final product.

Did the writing of Blonde *change your own view of Norma Jeane Baker?*

OATES: Ultimately, I didn't think of Norma Jeane as an isolated, idiosyncratic individual signifying nothing but herself, a specimen without a species; I came to think of her as a universal figure. I certainly hope that my portrait of her transcends sex and gender, and that male readers can identify as readily with her as female readers. But I don't recommend, for anyone, writing a psychologically realistic novel about any "historic" individual who is said to have committed suicide. It's just too . . . painful.

"JCO" AND I

(*After Borges*)

It is a fact that, to that other, nothing ever happens. I, a mortal woman, move through my life with the excited interest of a swimmer in uncharted waters—my predilections are few, but intense—while she, the other, is a mere shadow, a blur, a figure glimpsed in the corner of the eye. Rumors of "JCO" come to me third-hand and usually unrecognizable, arguing, absurdly, for her historical existence. But while *writing* exists, *writers* do not—as all writers know. It's true, I see her photograph—*my* "likeness"—yet it is rarely the same "likeness" from photograph to photograph, and the expression is usually one of faint bewilderment. *I acknowledge that I share a name and a face with "JCO,"* this expression suggests, *but this is a mere convenience. Please don't be deceived!*

"JCO" is not a person, nor even a personality, but a process that has resulted in a sequence of texts. Some of the texts are retained in my (our) memory, but some have bleached out, like pages of print left too long in the sun. Many of the texts have been translated into foreign languages, which is to say into texts at another remove from the primary—sometimes even the author's name, on the dust jacket of one of these texts, is unrecognizable by the author. I, on the contrary, am fated to be "real"—"physical"—"corporeal"—to "exist in Time." I continue to age year by year, if not hour by hour, while "JCO," the other, remains no fixed age—in spiritual essence, perhaps, forever poised between the fever of idealism and the chill of cynicism, a precocious eighteen years old. Yet, can a process be said to have an age?—an impulse, a strategy, an obsessive tracery, like planetary orbits to which planets, "real" planets, must conform?

No one wants to believe this obvious truth: the "artist" can inhabit any individual, for the individual is irrelevant to "art." (And what is "art"?—a firestorm rushing through Time, arising from no visible source and conforming to no principles of logic or causality.) "JCO" occasionally mines, and distorts, my personal history; but only because the history is close at hand, and then only when some idiosyncrasy about it suits her design, or some curious element of the symbolic. If you, a friend of mine, should appear in her work, have no fear—you won't recognize yourself, any more than I would recognize you.

It would be misleading to describe our relationship as hostile, in any emotional sense, for she, being bodiless, having no existence, has no emotions: we are more helpfully defined as diamagnetic, the one repulsing the other as magnetic poles repulse each other, so that "JCO" eclipses me, or, and this is less frequent, I eclipse "JCO," depending upon the strength of my will.

If one or the other of us must be sacrificed, it has always been me.

And so my life continues through the decades . . . not connected in the slightest with that conspicuous other with whom, by accident, I share a name and a likeness. The fact seems self-evident, that I was but the door through which she entered—"it" entered—but any door would have done as well. Does it matter which entrance you use, to enter a walled garden? Once you're inside, and have closed the door?

For once not she, but I, am writing these pages. Or so I believe.

ACKNOWLEDGMENTS

"District School #7 . . ." originally appeared, in a different form, in *Washington Post Book World* (1997).

"First Loves . . ." originally appeared in *American Poetry Review* (1999).

"To a Young Writer" originally appeared in *Letters to a Young Writer* edited by Frederick Busch (1999).

"Running and Writing" originally appeared in the *New York Times* (1999).

"What Sin to Me Unknown . . ." originally appeared, in a different form, in *Where I've Been, and Where I'm Going: Essays, Reviews, and Prose* (1999).

"Notes on Failure" originally appeared in *The Profane Art* (1973).

"Inspiration!" and "The Enigmatic Art of Self-Criticism" originally appeared, in different forms, in *(Woman) Writer: Occasions and Opportunities* (1988).

ACKNOWLEDGMENTS

"Reading as a Writer: The Artist as Craftsman" originally appeared in *On Writing Short Stories* edited by Tom Bailey (2000).

"The Writer's Studio" originally appeared in *American Poetry Review*, 2003.

"*Blonde* Ambition: Greg Johnson Interviews Joyce Carol Oates" originally appeared in *Prairie Schooner*, 2002. Reprinted with permission from Greg Johnson, 2003.

"'JCO' and I" originally appeared in *Antaeus* (1994).